Thanks to:

David Jnr
Jim and Hilda Murray
Micky and Mary Rooney
Our brothers and sisters
All of the Boat Club members
World Cruising Association,
and all on Arc 2000
Paul and Mike,
Bobby and Eric,
John and Margaret

Written in the middle of the night

Where does life start?
Where does life end?
It starts with ambition
But you need a good friend
As I sit here crossing
The Atlantic Ocean
In a small sailing boat
In a rolling motion
In 25 knots of wind and
A mast full of sail
I am 6'1 and feel very frail
The 20 foot waves look so tall
And me and my boat are very small
I see 30 foot whales
That rule this place
And although very scared
Bring a smile to my face
The stars at night
Play a wonderful game
And for thousands of miles
It all looks the same
It throws me to the left
And it throws me to the right
But I know it is just this ocean
Displaying it's awesome might
There is no place on earth
Like this deep deep blue
And now I know life only ends
When you want it to.

We are now crossing the Atlantic Ocean on Ciao Moody, a small sailing boat, completing my latest ambition. I am thinking what shall I do next? As you read on you will find I have done lots of funny things. Some beyond belief. But let me tell you everything in this book is true. Hard times, good times, sad times, the crazy things I have done. I think I must be crazy to have an ambition to write a book when I can't read and write properly, as you will find from this book. I know now that we can do anything we want to, if we are prepared to try. As I am a very adamant person I thought I would write what I want and not have it written for me - the proper way. I am sure this will keep you amused, but I have always done things my way. I was in Croatia last year, with a friend of mine, on a sailing boat and you know the way it is. After a few drinks you start telling each other the things that have happened to you in the past. My friend said "You have some great stories why don't you write a book?" So I suppose there is no better place to start than five days out at sea and sixteen days to go to the Caribbean.

Down wind in a rolling sea....

ciaomoody.com

I am not very clever
And I don't read and write
But I am full of ambition
And am very, very bright

IT'S FUNNY
BUT IT'S TRUE

It all started one day when I was looking through Auto Mart for a car and I started to read the section with the boats for sale. Yes I'm sure you know the feeling, basically day dreaming. But one boat caught my eye: it was a 21ft long day boat with a V8, 6.75 litre, three stage Hamilton Jet with a thruster plate to make it go in reverse.

I had never looked at boats before and this sounded like a good boat (toy), so I rang and got some details from the man who was selling it. Looking back now I bought a heap of rubbish. But that was the one that got us started. Well as you can imagine when I went home and told Colette about buying a boat she went absolutely ballistic at first, but I knew she would calm down after a bit and finally, she agreed to come and have a look at it with me. So off we went to Preston. The man who was selling it told me "All you have to do is put the lever forward to go forwards and back to go back". He said he would deliver it home for us so that was it, home it came. What we didn't know was that it would use eight gallons of petrol an hour and do 50 knots. From the first time in the water we had nothing but trouble. As it turned out, the motor had been frozen that winter and the heads were cracked. But now I know its all part of learning to sail. We lived on a small farm just outside Liverpool at the time and could only get out on a Sunday. So we loaded up the car and went to Carr Mill Dam with our pride and joy. When we got there the dam keeper was horrified. When he saw the size of the jet sticking out the back he told us "There is no way that thing can go on here" and to "Take it to the sea". So back home we went. We made some enquiries that week and were told to try Windermere in the Lake District. Next Sunday, off we went again. Half way up the motorway the boat started swerving all over the road and soon we were going from the outside lane to the hard shoulder and back. Thankfully nothing hit us. As you can imagine Colette and our son David, who at the time was only five, were beginning to hate sailing and we hadn't been on the water yet. We now know that when ever we tow a boat we need to use a stabilizer. We turned a lot of heads when we drove down the hill in to Bowness. We finally found our way to the wardens office and registered the boat etc. We put the boat on the water for the first time and put the car and trailer in the car park for the day. What happened next has been talked about on Lake Windermere ever since.

Well, as I said, the man who sold me the boat said all you have to do is put the lever forwards to go forward and backwards to go backwards. So I untied the only two pieces of string that I had holding it to the jetty and put the lever full forward and off we went at just on 50 knots right through the centre of Bowness Bay and all the way to Ambleside in about four minutes. Five minutes later the wardens arrived shouting and bawling at the top of their voices. They were very red faced and very angry. But we did not know what we had done wrong. We were just starting to enjoy sailing. We now know that there is a six mile an hour limit in the bay. We well and truly broke that bylaw. The warden was a very understanding guy and, when he finally calmed down, he saw the funny side. I'm just glad nobody was in the way. As we had just had our first flying lesson down the lake, we had very quickly burnt off all our fuel and went to refill at Windermere Aqautics. This is where we first saw people who were staying on their boats over the weekend. That sounded better than having to tow this damn great thing all the way back home to do it all again next week. We were allowed to rent a berth there and the change in our lives began. I don't think we had ever laughed so much as a family as we did that day and we hadn't got to the skiing episode yet. We bought six warps and fenders to replace our two pieces of string and I think we were starting to get to like sailing. We learnt so many things that day and laughed all the way back home. I don't think I had ever bought so much petrol in one day in all my life. We were convinced the boat must have a petrol leak. But that was the job for next week. As I said, at this time, we were living on a small holding, which had always been one of our ambitions, but this did not give us the fun we had on the boat. The three of us were very keen to get back the following week. This new obsession was taking a hold at a very early stage. I was also one of the owners of a very successful business at which I was spending 70 hours a week working with my two partners. As I drove home that day I knew our lives were about to change.

When we got home all we talked about that week was the boat. We went back the following Sunday and did the same all over again. We started to look at the inside to see if we could maybe sleep on her in the future. Down one small step and you were in the cabin and in the V there was a seat/berth on either side. We decided we would make a piece of wood to go in the middle, have some cushions made and this would be our bed. This was done over the next couple of weeks. Oh, and there wasn't a petrol leak, it just used 8 gallons an hour. We decided to get another person to help at the farm to give us more time at the boat. By the way the boat was called, "Sea Ye

Later". When I say more time, I was still working 6 days per week and alternate Sundays. We were opening new garages at a rate of one per year, and at this point, had six. Up until now my only thing in life had been work and making money. We were making a fair amount of money and Colette and I were investing it in property. That seemed to be the way to go in the late eighties. But my new found obsession was biting even harder. We went to the boat for the first time on a Saturday night after work. Colette had been shopping and had bought all kinds of things for the boat, pots, pans etc. Our bed was very small but, at the time, our son David was only about 4 feet tall. So I made a bunk for him across our bed and we slept under him. We were well on into the summer now and looking forward to our first holiday on the boat. We purchased a porta loo from a caravan place and now it was like a small home. It was also a bit similar to work as I was always fixing the engine and other things. The boat was full of lessons for me. I remember one day I decided to fix an old bilge pump that a previous owner had fitted. After reading a little about them I decided to strip it down, clean it, free the rust and thought it would probably work again. I undid the three screws holding it in place. I thought they were a bit long but carried on. The pump was also stuck down with some kind of silicone. I pulled at the pump and, eventually, it came off with three jets of water squirting up and into the boat. Someone had put the screws right through the bottom of the boat. I was frantically trying to put the screws back into the holes, but have you ever seen how much water comes in through a small hole in the bottom of a boat-never mind three holes! After a mad half hour, the man on the fork lift truck at the marina, told me to get the boat over to the slip and he lifted the back end of the boat out so I could get the screws back in the holes. Ever since that day I have always been very careful removing any screws out of the floor of boats, you don't know who's been there before you.

One of my partners in the business had just become a born again Christian and asked if we were in agreement about closing the garages on a Sunday. At this point I was ready to go to a 5 day week and have the weekends off to go to Windermere. This first season was going so fast, we were always laughing and there was always something going wrong or we were doing wrong. I remember one day, we were coming back into the marina. The boat had a flap on the jet that flapped over the end of the water jet and reversed the thrust. So, manoeuvring into the marina space I went into reverse and revved up hard as normal, looking behind me. The boat just carried on going forward at full speed, straight into the wall. What we didn't know was that the flap had fallen off during the day. I think people were starting to get used to our acts of comedy and I still haven't told you about the water skiing yet. Now that I was not working on Saturdays or Sundays we started to go up to the boat on a Friday night after work. It was expensive to keep the boat at the marina and being able to use it most weekends during the season was good and we had great fun. People started to talk about laying their boats up at the end of the season but we thought we'd only just got started. We arranged to take "Sea Ye Later" home to the small holding to rebuild the engine during the winter months. Because we were not at home at weekends we had started to reduced the livestock and had someone come in at weekends to see to what we had left. It seems hard to believe, looking back, that a boat could change all our plans. If you are just starting out, believe me, it will do the same to you. I was still doing my fair share at work and working very hard during the week. But I was conscious that my whole conversation was sailing and I was spending a lot of time reading about sailing too. Reading was something I had never done before. It may surprise you that I left school at thirteen years of age and could not read and write properly. I still do not spell too good, but Colette is a good speller. It is a fact that all the crew on board have to have different attributes.

I remember one day in work at the St. Helens depot, a man came in from Lytham St. Annes. He had a problem with his car. As I was fixing it for him, again out came the word boat. It turned out he was an old sea dog and sailed out of St. Annes. Although our type of boating was worlds apart and St. Helens is nowhere near the water, this led to our first visit to the sea. The man asked me and my family to come to his house on Sunday to talk about going on a trip to the Isle of Man. When I went home and told Colette, this went down like a lead balloon. "There is no way I am going on the sea". But when she calmed down I persuaded her just to go and meet the man on Sunday. Well we got there on time, as planned. It was an old wooden boat with no floor boards, just a bare hull painted black and red with hammock-type beds and a bucket in the corner. When we asked the question, "what happens if the weather gets rough?" The answer was, "We will go down below, batton down the hatches, get out the accordion and the whiskey and have a good old sing song". As you can imagine, we were not going to sea then, but something about it started me thinking. Colette and David were definitely put off. (I don't know whether it was the sing song or the bucket). So, back we went to the lake for a new season. But I was always thinking about the man going to sea in his old boat. I started to buy lots of other things; life jackets, flares and even an outboard motor which I fitted to the day boat. The new season was going well. We had rebuilt the old engine during the winter and had done lots of other work and now the boat was looking really good. I was secretly getting her ready to go to sea. One Saturday morning we were in the marina with lots of smoke coming out of the boat. When a lady came over and asked if we were on fire. I casually replied "no, it's just Colette cooking the breakfast". She could not believe it and sat watching and laughing. The lady was from the L.D.B.C. (Lake District Boat Club). She told us it was Open Day and invited us to come and have a look at the club house. We went and it looked good, so we joined. It is a mixed boat club with power and sail boats and there were lots of like minded people, just laughing and enjoying boating, especially when I told them some of our stories from the previous year.

I think the funniest was the day we tried to water ski. We arrived at the boat nice and early one day with my sister, Kath and Brother-in-Law, Peter to have a day out on the boat. After we had been up and down the lake a few times on this beautiful day we noticed there were a lot of people out water skiing. Peter asked if I'd ever tried it. I told him "No I don't know anything about it". Peter said he had seen it on the television and it looked easy. So off we went to the chandlers and bought a wet suit, some skis, ski rope and even a black rubber hat. Peter put all this on and said we had to back up close to the shore and he would get out onto the grass and put the skis on. You can imagine how he looked with his black rubber hat on. He went further back into the field until the rope was tight and I was to drive off as fast as I could. He said that as I drove off he would jump up. Well he did jump up, but then went flat on his face and I dragged him down the field on his nose. There were lots of people watching; I think they thought we were some kind of stunt act. When Peter got up off the floor, covered in cow muck, we were wetting ourselves laughing. Especially when he said, " I nearly did it, let's try again". So we did and I dragged him on his nose again. Well guess who turned up then. Yes, the lake warden. He was not happy. He just said, "what are you trying to do, kill him?"

On a Sunday morning the yachts would race at the club. It would always look very boring; they would only do about 3-4 miles per hour. One day one of the lads at the club was short of crew and asked if I would like to go with him. It was an E-boat called 'Eventually'. It's funny now looking back, my boat was called 'Sea Ye Later' and his was 'Eventually'. This was the first sail boat I had ever sailed on and all I did was get sent from side to side and thrown all over the place. It seemed like a life time. It took about 4 hours to do what I could have done in my boat in about 10 minutes. When I got back to the club house I said to Colette "Never again. That's the last sail boat I ever go on". How wrong that statement turned out to be. About six weeks later another member asked me to crew for him. After the last time, sailing was not for me. His boat was a Moody 33 centre cockpit and he said it was nothing like the E-boat. In fact, he was not only asking me to go sailing, he was asking Colette and David as well. We agreed to go the next day and that was it, I got the bug. We thoroughly enjoyed the day and I remember saying to Colette that I would like a boat like that and to go to sea.

I started sailing every week on that boat and was learning more and more. As the season came to an end I wanted our own sail boat. I put 'Sea Ye Later' up for sale and started looking for a yacht. I found a boat called 'Minnie Ha Ha'. It was standing in the car park at the marina where it had stood for two years. It was a Marcon Tomahawk 25ft with a fin keel. But we had to wait until our boat was sold and as we were right at the end of the season it was not going to sell very easily. We ended up taking it home again for the winter. By now the obsession had taken over and we decided to sell the farm house and buy a house that we could leave at weekends and during school holidays. We sold the farm and moved to a house in Warrington. At the beginning of the new season 'Sea Ye Later' sold and 'Minnie Ha Ha' was finally ours. We could now call ourselves sailors. Well, lake sailors. Our new boat was in good condition and all we had to do was clean her up and learn to sail her. I was trying to gather as much information about sailing as I could from everyone I met. But the only way you can learn is to keep making mistakes. Anyone who thinks they are doing it all right, all the time, has never sailed. I was talking and reading more and more about the sea. People were always telling us bad, horrendous stories about their friends who had gone to sea and the advantages of staying on the lake. That summer went very fast and I think we sailed at every possible opportunity. David had settled well into his new school and was getting very good results. Because we now went to Windermere straight from school on a Friday afternoon and stayed till early Monday morning most weekends, all David's friends were in Windermere. Warrington was really only a mid week base. That season was also packed with funny events. One we remember well, was when we were asked to join in a race. It was the

first time we had ever entered a race on our own boat.
Right from the start I wasn't very good at racing and
we still can't understand how people can shout and bawl,
and call each other awful names, and then stand and drink
together at the bar afterwards. Colette hated racing from
that very first race. What happened was, we were right at
the back of the fleet and all of the other boats had just
about finished. It was a club line finish with lots of people
looking out of the club house windows. The wind had
increased and I could not get the boat to point up enough
to get over the finish line. I tried about three times
but kept making a mess of the tacks. We could see all the
people in the club howling with laughter but I was
determined to finish that race. Colette had had enough
with me shouting at her and went down below. In the end,
I apologised to her and asked her to come up and help me
finish this race. Reluctantly, she agreed and started up the
stairwell. Just at that point the boat broached and the main
sheet wrapped around Colettes' neck. As the boom came
crashing across it nearly ripped off her head. Well, we did
finish that race and, needless to say we came last. But we
still got a big round of applause when we came into the
club house. I always remember, when we got in, Colettes'
pony tail was on the front of her head and she had bright
red marks around her neck. Everyone thought we had been
fighting. The big lesson we learnt that day was that we

would never sail again without fitting a boom preventor. I think we were just very very lucky that Colette had not been seriously injured.

We went on racing for a few more years but we were never very keen. With joining the boat club we seemed to be spending less time on the lake and more time in the club. I suppose this is the downside to all boat clubs, but on the other hand, you learn a lot by talking to other people. The club had arranged an annual trip to the London Boat Show and we were very keen to go. While we were at the show, one of the club members asked if we fancied going on a flotilla holiday with him and his family. They had a young girl the same age as our son. This sounded like a good way to get on the sea for the first time. We arranged to go to Yugoslavia (now Croatia). Well, at long last we were going to sail on salt water for the first time. The only problem was we didn't know anything about navigation. But the man we were going with had a basic understanding and after all we were going in a flotilla. We hired a 40 foot plus boat with wheel steering, so right away that was something new. The flotilla we were with had fun races each day and we really enjoyed them. Unfortunately, the boom got in the way again. We had just left Split marina and were sailing along nicely when in the distance I saw a very fast boat coming towards us. I said to my friend, "Can you see that boat". He replied "Yes, but power gives way to sail". I, not knowing any different at the time, simply said, "O.K." A few minutes later I said, "This boat is coming right towards us." My friend replied again in a slightly higher tone of voice "Power gives way to sail." This time I knew we were not in a good position. I might not have been able to sail very well but I knew that when 10,000 tons of steel is bearing down on you at 20 knots, it was time you got out of the way. I then shouted "He is going to hit us" and my friend threw the wheel over fast. Unfortunately, the boom hit me on the back of the head, knocking me to the floor. The boat turned out to be a very large warship that was going very fast. I am sure if we hadn't moved when we did it would definitely have run us down. And yes, power should give way to sail, but, does he have the ability to manoeuvre, is he restricted by his draught, has he seen you, is there anyone on watch? My lesson that day was to get out of the way. And really, no matter whose boat you are on, fit a boom preventor.

When we returned to England a week later, I went to the doctors with bad headaches. They said that I was still concussed and I was very lucky that I had not cracked my skull or had my neck broken. All in all, we had a good holiday and Colette and I said we would go back to Yugoslavia as it was such a beautiful place. Unfortunately, the war started only weeks after we returned home and most of the flotilla companies and private boats left that area.

When we got back to England, it was the start of our fourth season and we found that we were only going out on a Sunday morning to race and then going back to the club. To some extent, although we were enjoying it, we were starting to miss the sailing, the time on the water and nights on the anchor just sitting watching the sun go down. I was getting more and more determined to go to the sea now and Colette was starting to think about it as well. We went and looked at Preston, Fleetwood, Maryport and Liverpool. These ports would have meant moving the boat on a low loader and David was very happy at Windermere, so once again, we were to stay on the lake. We started getting very involved in the club and the racing although we were never very good. We decided maybe we should have a faster boat. So we sold 'Minnie Ha Ha' and bought a Trapper 300 called 'Why Knot'. We resigned ourselves to staying on the lake for a few more years. I became a member of the committee and we spent more and more time in the club. I was drinking more than I had ever drunk before and this was not what we had set out to do. We were getting more and more trapped. I seemed to be spending my time working in the club. We went to the

Boat Show again, this time we booked to go to Turkey. That was a club/flotilla type of holiday. This meant that you could sail on toppers, windboards, hobbycats, lasers and a small boat called an Explorer. They also had a small fleet of 32's. In our usual fashion we even managed to get ourselves into a mess there. We went out around a small bay in one of the Explorers with some other people for lunch. It was decided that we would have a small race back but somehow we sailed right past the bay where the club was at Yedi Buku. We sailed for about two hours. Yes, you've guessed it, we were lost. No flares, no water, no food, no charts and the sun beating down on us. Luckily the ferry came past coming the other way and we realised we were on our way to Greece. We turned around and followed the ferry back arriving about three hours later with everyone out looking for us. Well we all had a good laugh about it that night in the bar. I know now how important it is to keep enjoying, laughing and having fun whilst you are sailing. If you can't make mistakes and laugh about them you may as well give up. David was now coming to an age when he had to move school again, to the seniors. He was doing very well and getting top results, so whichever school he went to now, he would have to stay at. I considered selling my share of the business and moving to Scotland so we could sail on the Clyde, but we were unsure of schooling. There was a very good secondary school in

Windermere and David already had lots of friends there, so we mad a decision to buy a house in the Lakes and sold our house in Warrington. I drove 200 miles to work and back, everyday.

 We had been up to Scotland a few times, sailing on charter boats with some other club members and were starting to like salt water sailing. But we had never been to sea on our own. I still did not know anything about navigation, but I knew we were getting closer to going. We decided that what we needed was a trailer sailer and someone suggested a Hunter Sonata as this was a good racing boat/weekender. We started looking and found one in Helensburgh in Scotland. It was called "Polymer" and we bought it. We trailed her back to Windermere. We said we would race her for a short time on the lake and then go to Scotland. What I never realised was the more I was shouting at Colette and David when we were racing, the more I was putting them off sailing all together. Within that year Colette and David stopped racing. I think it was a mixture of things. We now had a beautiful home in Windermere with lots of gardens. I was a bad skipper, always shouting and bawling and getting excited over stupid things. David was happy to stay in at the weekends as he had his friends there, his computer and other things

to keep him occupied. I started racing on a Sunday with two lads from the club. Colette and David stayed at home and then met me in the club house for lunch. At that time I thought that this was the end of us sailing as a family. I was also made Rear Commodore at the L.D.B.C, so the dreams of going to sea were getting further away. I find that there is no better person in the world to sail with than your wife. Please learn to sail without shouting, don't put her off as I did. Although Colette had stopped sailing on the lake I still thought that there was a slim chance that she might come with me to Scotland. I had been up there that year with some friends for a week, but sailing was not the same without Colette. It was the first time we had ever been away from each other (we had been together fifteen years at that time). I have to tell you that if I ever had to make the choice between sailing and my wife, I would give up sailing. (Well I think I would!).

Now that we had virtually stopped sailing, I had quite a lot of free time and I thought this would be a good time to learn navigation. I went and did a Coastal Skipper theory course at the college in Ambleside.

I thought that if I learnt navigation and tried to learn how to be a better skipper on a boat I would be able to get Colette back to the water. I knew that David would not come back to sailing for a few years, he has a very strong mind of his own. He was doing well at school, well at football and karate, but I knew that when he was ready he would sail again. Most of my family and friends thought I was mad when I told them I was going to college to learn navigation. The man that was running the course was an old sea dog with a lot of stories to tell and this was just what I needed. But I didn't know what I was letting myself in for. The time I went to college was the first time I had been in a classroom since I was 13 and I felt like a duck out of water.

Most of the people on the course had a basic under-standing, but I didn't have a clue. For the first two hours they were talking about latitudes, longitudes, variation, deviation, degrees, miles and minutes. I sat there waiting for the break time so that I could go home, as it was all over my head. I had paid for the course in advance to the R.Y.A., so I thought if I telephoned them the next morning and explain that I had made a big mistake they would probably give me a refund or a credit that I could maybe use later or sell to someone else. As I sat there I was thinking that this was definitely the end of our sailing life. Well eventually the tea break came and I thought I had better tell the teacher I was going home. So as soon as the break came he went straight outside for a smoke. Most of the rest of the class went to the coffee machine. This gave me a chance to talk to him on my own. I explained that I had made a mistake and I did not understand. He asked me which part I did not understand and I said all of it. He asked me not to go and to stick it out until the end of the day. After the break he gave us all the R.Y.A package. This included demonstration charts and the course syllabus. At the end of the day I went to him, to give him back the package. He asked me what I would do if I were caught in a gale. I replied that I would reef down as much as possible, clip all my crew on and head out to safe water. He said, "Good I didn't think you were the type to give up and die". I tried to explain I wasn't just giving up. It was all just over my head. He explained that the whole of navigation and safety at sea was originally put together by seafarers not brain surgeons or wise kids. He asked me to take the package home, have a look at it for a few days and ring him at home in Kendal if there was anything I did not understand. I could see the guy did not want me to give up. Well I took the package and locked myself in my office for about 3 days. But I still could not grasp it at all. I took the man at his word and rang him up. He invited me to his house the next day. I spent most of the day with him and he showed me how easy it really is. I think I was just trying too hard.

Once I got an understanding of latitude and longitude and compass variation the rest was just a picture on the chart. With regards to tide, I have always been quite good at figures so I found this very easy. I continued the course with determination and actually passed with top marks. Please do not be put off by the start of one of these courses, as once you get into it and get a basic understanding, it is very straightforward and easy. If I can pass it so can you. One thing I would say about the theory course is, if you don't keep up with it after you have passed, you will very quickly forget it. I knew now that I had to get on the sea as quickly as I could so I could put it all into practice. So I booked a one week, day skipper practical course in Scotland and passed.

Back at the club, a new year was starting and I was Rear Commodore. Unfortunately, the club racing was doing nothing for me then; I was fed up with sailing Windermere. I have to say though, it is an excellent place to learn to sail. The Sonata Nationals were being held at Scotland that year. I decided to enter 'Polymer' and go with the crew in one of the races. We actually got a third . This was a very good result for us, we had a very good week. But it was not with Colette and that was what I really wanted. So, I had an idea. I would leave the boat in Scotland. That way we would have to go back up to pick it up. I thought we could have a week there as a family. When I got home we made plans to go to Scotland in a few weeks time when there was a school holiday. I was really looking forward to this holiday just to show Colette and David all that I had learnt in the last year. I spent every night on the chart table at home doing all the trips we were going to make. I had done the tides for every day we would be there. David was a little bit reluctant about going but I promised him we would not do too much sailing. We would stop off at different places for a couple of days.

The day came when we were finally going to go to the sea. We loaded up the car with all our food etc, and set off for Scotland. At this time I was under quite a lot of pressure at work and it was about a 200 mile journey to Inverkip where I had left the boat. On the way up there Colette and I were having a dispute, something to do with work, and the rain was absolutely pouring down. This was not the start I wanted for this holiday. By the time we got to the boat we were having heated words. We had just finished putting all the food and gear on the boat , we were absolutely soaked and one word led to another. I lost my temper and said "That's it we're going home". So, we got back in the car and drove all the way back to Windermere. A round trip of 400 miles. We went back the next day and picked up the boat. I was very disappointed. I put the boat back on the lake, didn't bother sailing for a month or two and we were both ready to call sailing a day. But I was still getting a lot of sailing magazines delivered to the house and Colette would enjoy reading them. One day I got home from work and she told me it was Cowes Week in a few weeks time on the Isle of Wight. I had never sailed on the Solent before and I had heard that there was a big tide to contend with, but I was still keen to go and Colette was about 50/50. David said as long as we didn't drive all the way there just to drive all the way back again, he didn't mind. I promised David and Colette that if we weren't enjoying it when we got there, we would book into a hotel, sell the boat when we got home and give up for good.

At this stage, I was about to tell you what happened at Cowes. But first I thought I would tell you this. This morning I got up at around 7.15 Eastern Caribbean Time, as I am in St. Martin at Simpson Bay Marina. I switched on the VHF radio on Channel 14. I was told by a man in the local boat club (oh no, not another boat club), that Channel 14 VHF is the local cruiser net: It is very good; you can buy and sell things, get the weather and hear what is going on around St. Martin. Well, believe it or not, the first thing I heard was that there was a writer's meeting at one of the local bars at 10 o'clock. At this point I had not told anyone I was writing a book, so I thought that this was a good point in the book to find out if I was wasting my time or not. So I went to the meeting.

There were about six other people there and, at first I thought, "I am in the wrong place here". They were talking about books that different people had written and I didn't have a clue what they were talking about. In fact, a man walked past me and someone said "Oh that's so and so, I forget the name", and I said "Oh right". He said "You know who so and so is" and I said "I'm sorry I don't" and he told me he had written about thirty books. You should have seen his face when I told him I didn't read books. It was a great meeting. People read different things out that they had written and I was asked what I had written. When I told them that I don't read and write too well and just write it down as best I can at night and Colette puts it on the computer the next day, they thought it was great. I was asked how many words I had to date. I told them I had about 7,500 so far. They told me I was doing well, and asked if this was from the beginning of my life. I said "No, this was from the start of my sailing life". One of the suggestions that came out of the meeting was that I should drop back a bit and tell the reader where I have come from..... so hold tight, here we go.

I was born in Liverpool in 1957 in a street called Myrtle Street in the city centre. My Mother and Father had three daughters before me so I was the first and only boy. Our house in Myrtle Street was a shop and we lived behind and above it. Both my parents worked in the shop seven days a week to keep us four kids in a good lifestyle. We were known as a posh family because we had a car and I was sent to a private school. It was my Mothers intention that I was to be a doctor. I was taken every day to school in the car with a full uniform, blazer, short pants and a cap and I was never allowed to play out at home with the local kids. I would always have to come home and study. I remember my mother was always taking headache tablets (I can remember us all going on holiday to Jersey), but only my father knew that my mother was very ill. Not long after we came back, my mother died of a brain haemorrhage. This was the biggest tragedy to ever hit our family. They say that the first cut is the deepest. I still believe that to this day and I don't think there is ever a day goes by without me thinking about her. I was nine years of age when she died and my father had some big decisions to make.

He had the shop to run, three teenage daughters and me. There was no way he could continue to take me to the private school every day in the car as there was no one to mind the shop. He didn't want to continue with the shop long term; he wanted to go back to the tools. He used to be a carpenter/joiner. But, he wouldn't have the money to send me to that school. He made a very hard decision and sent me to the local school and allowed me to play out with the local kids in the street. He knew he was taking a very big chance. I would learn to look after myself or fall by the way side. I remember a very sad but funny story. I was not a violent child and had never had to fight. I was out one day and two boys were hitting me. I ran into the shop to tell my dad. The shop was full of people so he sat me on the back stairs and I will never forget what he said. He said "Your mother has gone now. You must go back out and sort the boys out yourself". I now know that it was breaking his heart to say it, but he knew he had to make me independent. I went down the stairs to the cellar, went to my Dad's tool box and got out the big wooden mallet. I put it behind my back and went out into the street. The two boys came over to me laughing and shouting, so I promptly whacked them both over the head with the mallet. Just once each and they were both on the floor. Nobody ever picked on me again and I knew that nothing would ever get in my way, for the rest of my life.

Unfortunately, I became a bad lad at school and would not settle. I was always fighting and in the end I was asked to leave at 13 years of age. I got a job in a clothes shop (boutique) in Liverpool, in the stock room, but unfortunately got involved in smoking drugs and things. I was going nowhere, just running up more and more debt. I was very fortunate to meet some new friends who turned out in later years to be my business partners. I got a job as an exhaust fitter and paid off my debts. I enjoyed my new job, was eager to learn and I was very good at it. With my two friends, I bought a mobile disco and after a few years of being a DJ in the evenings, I was very confident. I then became determined we should have our own exhaust centres. I had met Colette one night after one of the discos, we later got married and David was born in 1980. I opened our first garage later that year. Well I had better get back and tell you about Cowes Week. Oh, by the way, I heard from David yesterday and he had just passed his third set of exams. He is studying to be a doctor. So, maybe there will be a Dr. David Murray after all!

O.K. So it was early July and we had the new car all loaded up with the Sonata and our little speed boat on the back. Our little speed boat was an Avon 345 Super Sport with a 30 hp Yamaha outboard. We managed to fit it under the Sonata. The back of the car was full to the top. It was a Landrover Discovery automatic and I had fitted a full set of reinforced, low profile tyres to the trailer. So we shouldn't have had any mechanical problems and of course we were using a stabiliser. We should have been able to stay in the lane we wanted without going all over the motorway. We had a great ride down to Southampton, absolutely trouble free. When we got there we put the whole rig on the car ferry. It looked quite funny, putting a boat onto the car ferry just to go to the Isle of Wight, when there was only about 5 miles to cross. But we wanted the car and the trailer on the other side as well. We finally arrived about 6 o'clock in the evening. It was a beautiful day and it would be light until about 9.30. So, I gave Colette and David the choice. We could go and find a hotel for the night or we could sleep on the boat on the hardstanding at the marina. I had made the saloon of the Sonata so that the two seats either side converted into one big double bed by putting a piece in the centre and David had the big berth at the front of the boat. They decided we would stay on the boat so that we could get put into the water bright and early the next day. We seemed to be back to laughing and joking, just getting up and down the ladder in the car park.

This was just like sailing used to be before it all became too serious. The next day both boats were put in the water and we got ourselves set up in a berth. We were enjoying every minute of it. We went out on the little boat the first day and had a good look at the Solent. We watched all the races starting. There were hundreds of boats there and the atmosphere was great. The weather was my big saviour as the sun was cracking the flags. The bars were full and the streets of Cowes were bustling with boat people of all kinds. The next day we went sailing. We planned out our route, plotted our course and went over every inch of the way. We looked up every mark, checked the tide times over and over again. You would think we were about to do an around the world passage, but we were just sailing to the River Hamble, which was about 10 miles away. We did it all with no mishaps. We sat that evening and did it all again. This time we were going to go up the River Beaulieu to the motor museum. We got there and had a great time. This is what we had been missing about sailing; just being together and having fun. There was no shouting and bawling, just a good old laugh, sitting out at night and having a quiet drink. There was no stopping us now. We decided we would plan to go out through the Needles and round to Christchurch. I knew I was taking a big chance because if I made a mess I would have put David and Colette off for good. But they too were happy to go ahead. At the time this was a hard passage to plan as we had to get out through the Needles with the tide and then make sure we went up the river to Christchurch on high water because there was only just enough depth for a Sonata with a fin keel. But we worked it all out to perfection (so we thought). Everything went well all the way to the top of the river. As we were going up the river, I thought I felt one or two little bumps on the keel, but then I thought this was, maybe, just a little bit of swell. Well as you can see, it was all going too well. That night we went into the Christchurch Yacht Club for a drink. While we were at the bar, the steward asked me what kind of boat we were sailing. I told him a Sonata. He said "It must be a bilge keeler, is it". I told him no, it was a fin keel. He looked at me quite shocked and said, "You got here today". I, feeling quite smart replied "Yes we worked out the tides and got up the river on the top of high water". He said "Very good are you staying a couple of weeks". I replied we were leaving tomorrow. He said "You're not, it was the last of Springs last night". I hadn't taken this into consideration. Yes, the bumps on the keel on the way up were us hitting the bottom. When we got back to the boat we started reading all the books and I worked out that the next high water was about 4.15 am. So we had a few hours sleep and said we would leave David in bed. We thought if we stick to the middle of the Channel we might just bounce our way out on high water. We were awakened by small fishing boats making their way out. So as planned, up and off we went. We would eat breakfast once we were out. We were going well for the first 15 minutes but then, we hit the bottom for the first time. We kept the speed on and managed to keep going. Then we hit again but this time a bit harder. Fortunately, again we bounced and kept going. We came to the last bend and I kept to the centre. There was a red buoy in front of me and I left it to Port, yes on my left hand side. Then bang, we were well and truly on the putty. Yes, you are right, I should have left the buoy to starboard, on my right hand side on the way out. Red to port on your way in, red to starboard on you way out. I will never make that mistake again! I revved our little outboard as much as I could and we leaned the boat over as much as we could. We tried everything, but unfortunately we had well and truly hit the bottom at about 5 knots. A small fishing boat that was coming past even tried to pull us off but he was also rushing to get out while he had enough water and, unfortunately, he could not make any difference. Well we sat and the sun came up and the water went down and down and down until we were on our side on the grass bank. If you are one of the tourists that took our picture that day, we would love a copy, as it must have made a perfect picture. The only good thing was we could see which way the keel was lying and which was the best way to get off when the water came back at Midday. Have you ever been on a boat on it's side? It is quite a weird feeling. The hatch is now at the side of the boat, the stairwell is now going sideways and trying to use the loo is something else!

Well something had to go wrong and at least I now knew what it was. Things on board were quite quiet really. We did not have a lot of food on board as we were only day sailing and eating out at night. We were not in any serious danger because we could have got off and walked to the bank. In fact there were people going past us walking their dogs. I am sure they were all going to get their cameras. Just before high water, a man in a motor sailer came past us. He said to be ready in about twenty minutes and that he would come back and help us get off. As good as his word the man came back. What he did was quite smart really: he whizzed around us shaking up the water and, as he did, I drove back into the Channel. He then got in front of us and kept speeding up and then slowing down. As he was disturbing the water, we managed to bump ourselves all the way out. We were so happy, the sun was still shining, and now we were seeing the funny side. But, what we never realised was that now the wind and tide were coming out of the Solent, through the Needles at 4 knots, and we were trying to sail against it. The people on the boats that were anchored just outside the Needles must have been laughing their heads off, watching us. We logged thirteen miles of tacking to cover two miles of water. Eventually, the tide turned. The only food we had on board by now was jam and bread. This being a traditional Scouse meal, jam butties kept us going. We got into Yarmouth harbour at 9.30 pm. Now that was a long day on a Sonata but we learnt so much that day. The next day, when we got up, I apologised to Colette and David, but they said "You only made one mistake with that red buoy". But I knew that I had made more than one mistake. I should have taken Neaps and Springs into consideration. I shouldn't have tried to beat the wind and tide. I should have put down my anchor.

You know, the six p's. *Poor-preparation-provides-piss-poor-performance.* The rest of that week went very well and we had a great time. All at the boat club were waiting for our stories when we got home. I think there were bets on whether Colette would ever go on a boat again or not. I had enjoyed the time on the boat with David and Colette so much that week, just cruising, that I made the decision that racing was not for me. I have a saying that is .. "Racing does for sailing what golf does to walking".

I am just reading from my log book and it says "It has been a great holiday and we will come back to the Solent again next year. Total miles on this trip 138".

 When we got back, I made it known that I was not going to race anymore and was going to look for a trailer sailer with a bilge keel. Two weeks after, a boat club member bought the Sonata from us. We spent the rest of the season at the boat club and going away looking at boats. Then, we found our first cruising boat. A Hunter Horizon, bilge keel called 'Slipaway'. It was in Exmouth in Devon. We had a six wheel trailer custom built for her and bought her back to Windermere. But only for a few weeks while we got to know her. Colette was happy to go sailing again. We were both looking forward to going cruising. David was still doing very well at school. I had totally lost interest in the business and I always said that the first day you get up and don't want to go to work is the day you should leave that job. As I was eating my breakfast, I told Colette that I was going to sell our share of the business. I had had enough. She was very shocked but she also knew that I was not happy there and that what used to be a good laugh with my two mates had become a real business. I was not prepared to let it change my character or my way of life.

So I sold out in March 1996. But, because there were a lot of loose ends to tie up with the business, and I was also Vice Commodore at the boat club, it was still going to be a busy year for us.

Just before I start the next section, I have just boarded an aeroplane at St. Martin Airport and am waiting to take off. It is an American Airline jet 757 to San Juan. I have never had this much leg room before! The reason I am on this flight is because we can not sail any further without getting an American visa. My sister lives in Florida and some of my family are flying out today from the U.K. to see her. It was our plan to be there when they arrived. So we decided to fly and go to the Miami Boat Show at the same time. Remember if you are going to sail to the U.S. You must get a visa from the U.K. Order it in good time.

Back to the story. One of the first things that we had to master with 'Slipaway' was getting the mast up and down. We also had to make a single line reefing system so we could sail easily on our own. It didn't take very long to make the changes that we wanted to the boat and she was ready to go. Each year I had been away on a lads' week on one boat or another, so I decided that I would take 'Slipaway' to Scotland first. If I went with the lads for a week, we could get the mast up and get her rigged ready for Colette and David coming for a holiday, and oh, what a week we had!

We drove up from Windermere on Saturday and put the boat in the water at Inverkip. Our first plan was to go to Rothsey, about ten miles away. Now if you haven't been to Rothsey before it is hard to imagine. I believe that many years ago this was the Blackpool of Scotland. It was the place where all the Scots went for holidays. It has not had any money spent on it for years. But sailing boats are still made very welcome. We had a night out there and enjoyed the Scottish hospitality. The next day we sailed to East Loch Tarbet. Now this place was made famous by the McEwans' Race Week. When this race was on, the boats used to be rafted together, and there were so many boats that you could walk from one side of the marina to the other across them. But, thankfully, when we got there it was not that busy.

We went to one of the pubs on the quay and had our normal steak and chips for four. I remember that particular night, we were asked to leave about 12 o'clock. When we got outside I asked how much the bill was but nobody seemed to know. By this time we were back at the boat. We had to go back to the bar as we had not paid. I was knocking on the door, but they would not let us in. In the end I shouted through the letter box "I want to pay our bill". I don't think that door had ever been opened so fast! The man could not believe that he had let us go out owing him £80. He was then very fast to ask if we would like to stay for a drink! The next day we were off to Ardrishaig, which is the entrance to the Crinnan Canal.

The day after, we went through the canal. Now that is fun, but hard work. The following morning we sailed to the Isle of Jura. We will always remember the saying "You're all doomed". We arrived at around 4 hours after high water and we had about two metres of water outside the distillery. We got as close as we could so that the boat could stand down at low water. We went ashore to have egg and bacon at the hotel and do the distillery tour. It is a funny place. When we asked if there was somewhere we could leave our coats we were told "Yes, just leave them on the village green". There are not many places left in the world where you can do that and still have a coat to take home.

We were walking to the distillery when there was an old boy looking at the boat. It was him that just said "You are all doomed". He did not know it was a bilge keeler and, this time I knew I had my tides right. When we got back from the distillery trip and the tide was rising we left and went up Loch Sween. Now this was a night I will never forget. We got anchored down at about 4 o'clock in a place called Tayvallach. This is at the very top of Loch Sween. You can not go any further. We blew up the dinghy and arranged to go ashore and all agreed that we would go and find the telephones, showers, restaurants etc. We agreed that we would then go back to the boat and have a little sleep before going out for the evening. It is only a small place, so we split up. Two went one way and two went the other.

After about half an hour my friend and I could not find the other two. We thought that they must be in the pub. We went to have a look and oh yes, there they were standing with two pints of Caffreys bitter. Well you know the saying if you can't beat them join them. So, two more Caffreys please. Well, they were nice so it was four more Caffreys please, and four more and four more. Then we had to go and get washed, so we asked what time they served food until. We were told that last orders for food was 9 o'clock. Well, the laughing and the joking was not stopping and then it was four more and so on. After that I remember the barman saying "you will have to order your food now boys if you want to eat, it is 9 o'clock." O.K. steak and chips four times. We finally got out at about 1.30 in the morning. I remember the bill was £132 and the food was £29.50 of the bill. It was funny when we got back to the boat at around 2.30, it was a lovely night and one of the lads was hanging over the side. He was a bit ill. (I think it must have been the chips!!) But he was quite safe, we had his feet tied up with the main sheet and had him securely fastened around the winch. One of the other lads was making Stilton cheese on toast to accompany the bottle of Jura whisky that we had bought at the distillery. But the lad who was over the side did not want any. We just sat and laughed till the sun came up. We had a great week and were back in the club house for Saturday night. We left the boat at Inverkip. We had a good night at the club. However my friend who had refused the Stilton on toast, the one who had eaten too many chips, did not have a drink. In fact, he did not have a drink for about 6 weeks.

I still had a lot of things to sort out to do with the business, because part of the demerger I had done to sell our shares meant that we had to take some of the garages. So I was still having to run them until I could sell them off. This was keeping Colette very busy, as she was having to do all the purchasing, the paying of the bills, all the office work as well as having to do her normal work to do with our property company. With also being Vice Commodore of the boat club there was not a lot of time for sailing. But, as the weather was not very good early that year, it was not too bad. We made a plan to go to Scotland and have a look at the Crinnan Canal. We had a lot of good fun. Now we were beginning to see a lot of other people making mistakes, and there were lots of them. So, don't think that it is just you or me that makes them.

One day when we were going through the Crinnan Canal, there was a boat going through along side us. He was a shouter. He reminded me of how I used to be. He was screaming and shouting that much at his crew that the poor ladies on the boat were terrified. Every time he would throw them a rope, they were that frightened that they would drop it and the more he would shout. In the end we had to stop and let him go ahead of us, as we were laughing that much that I thought he was going to get angry with us.

Our David thought it was great fun. He was running down the side of the canal opening the lock gates. Every time he would drop down a rope he would always manage to land it on Colette's head. Although it was teaming down with rain that day, Colette was still managing to see the funny side as he was doing it on purpose. One of the things we learnt is that you must have a lot of long ropes (warps) and a lot of good heavy fenders, or even a few old tyres, when going through the locks. Just take your time and there is a great time to be had even in the canal. Now, at long last we were not making as many mistakes. We were starting to make longer trips and go out in heavier weather. I think this is the only way you learn, but remember, reef early. If you are thinking of putting a reef in, it is the time to do it. If you are thinking of taking a reef out, put the kettle on. That has always been our motto and I think that it is good practice to keep putting reefs in every time you go out at first. The more you do it the easier it becomes. It also takes away the fear from the crew. They will probably have a moan about all the work they have to do, but it will stop them getting bored and you will find it much easier to reef down when you have to with a good practiced crew.

The other thing I like to do is to throw a fender over the side and then simply say "I've gone, that's me in the water". Then just sit down and watch. If you do this enough times, you will be surprised how good your wife and crew become at the Man Overboard drill. It is great fun doing it with a fender. I hope we never have to do it for real.

We had a fabulous week and one of the things we talked about was to plan to do a Channel crossing. It sounded so far away, but I knew it would not be long before we would be trying it. We had a few more weeks up in Scotland and then brought the boat back to Windermere. The more we were going on the sea, the more we realised how much extra safety gear was needed. We were starting to look a bit strange now on Windermere as we were fitting Dan buoys, horseshoes, lifelines, off-shore flare packs, code flags and a fog horn. I think people must have thought we were mad when we would plot a course to Ambleside and practice dead reckoning. But, if you don't keep doing it you will forget how.

We used to plot Global Positioning Satellite waypoints to the race marks and then we would practice sailing to them. We would do compass bearings and cocked hats on the lake. We would sail between the islands and sail off the depth sounder into three metres just to practice sailing back out to deep water. Yes, we did hit the bottom sometimes, but if you never hit the bottom you wouldn't get any practice getting off. Obviously there is no tide on the lake so you have to do it by yourself. There is no high water to help you. It's all down to push and shove.

We had a funny time one day. We were at home and there had been some bad weather the night before and our boat had broken away from its mooring buoy. In fact it was one of the shackles low down on the chain that had broken and the boat had gone off on a little cruise of its own. Thankfully, it didn't hit anything but, eventually, it came to a stop at White Cross Bay on a nice big patch of mud. So, there was no damage. We got the phone call from the lake warden at 9 o'clock in the morning and all he said was "Your boat is on the beach at White Cross Bay". Well as this boat was 'Minnie Ha Ha' and she, as I said earlier, was a fin keel boat, we were expecting the worst. We were thinking it must be on its side, but no she was just standing there in that nice big patch of mud.

When we arrived in our dinghy we got on board and all was good. The first thing I tried was to drive it back out in reverse. She had a good little Yanmar 10 engine and it was running full-out in reverse. But the boat was not going to move. It had well and truly run aground.

Now, here's the funny bit. You know when somebody keeps saying something that you know for a fact won't work, well Colette was doing just that. She said to me "Why don't we go to the front in the dinghy and push". At first I just said "No you can't do that" but she went on and on. So in the end I said "Right, come on." So we got back into the dinghy and went to the front of the boat and Colette stood up and started to try to push the boat back. Well as the dinghy moved backwards, down she went flat on her face. "Now do you believe me, you can't push 3 ton of boat from an 8 foot dinghy!". And, once again, we were howling, laughing. I think we tried everything we could think of. We pushed it, we shoved it, we tried towing it backwards with the dinghy. Colette tried towing it while I was revving it up in reverse. A young lad in a very fast speed boat tried to tow us, but it was no good, it would not move. So, in the end, like everything else to do with boats, we learnt a very expensive lesson. We decided the only way to do it was to ring the professionals and ask them to help us. We had spent nearly 4 hours in the rain and had just about had enough. We rang one of the boat yards and told them our problem. "Yes sure we can do that for you, but you have to come and pay first, £150 plus

VAT". Well at that price, we thought, it was definitely going to be a big job. Anyway, we had no choice. We paid the bill and then a young lad about sixteen asked me to show him where the boat was. He followed us back. He was in a small rubber dinghy too. I thought he was just coming to see what equipment they needed to do the job. But no, he simply asked me to unclip the main halyard from the main sail and to pass the end to him. He tied it to a long rope and slowly moved off in his little rubber dinghy and, of course, with the leverage from the top of the mast, over she came ever so gently and obviously the keel came out of the mud. He then pulled us sidewards for about twenty metres into deep water, undid his rope, gave me back the main halyard and just said, "That's how you do it". The whole thing took him about three minutes from start to finish. So easy when you know how. I have since found that you can also do this by putting weight at the end of the boom and swinging it out to the side. It is a lot safer to put the crew in the dinghy and apply the weight to the end of the boom, than to have crew sitting out on the boom. Please remember when you are trying these different things, like getting hold of the shrouds and leaning out trapezing, moving weight around the boat, make sure that yourself and your crew are clipped on. The last thing you want is a man overboard with a boat that won't move. And the smart bums amongst you will say that if you are on the bottom you are in shallow water, and yes, I have to agree. But if you were on the bramble bank on the Solent for example, a non-swimmer in a three knot tide will be away before you know it. It doesn't even have to be a non-swimmer; a fully clothed good swimmer without a lifejacket on, in cold water would be very lucky to get back on board. Think safe and live to laugh about it later.

We enjoyed our time down in the Solent so much that we made plans to go back down and stay a few weeks this time. It was to follow our new dream, to cross the English Channel. We read all about the big nasty tides. But we knew it was the next thing to do. We loaded everything back up again and drove down to the Hamble River, where we put it all back in the water. We had a few days in the Solent and then went round to Christchurch and then on to Poole. From Poole to Cherbourg was about sixty three miles and we planned it over and over again. I spoke to as many people as I could to pick their brains. It was to be our big adventure. I thought it would be the longest trip we would ever do. We worked it all out; if we left at 4 o'clock in the morning we would arrive at Cherbourg in the daylight. Well, all set to go, up at 3.30 and it was raining, so we were frightened off by the poor visibility and went back to bed. The next day we did it all again, up at 3.30, it was foggy so back to bed. The next day, the forecast was 5-6 north east, we went back to bed. The truth was that we were a little apprehensive about going so far. The next day we got up at 3.30 and left. The forecast was north east 4-5, visibility good, so it was now or never.

When we got about five miles out there was a bit of fog moving across the Channel, but it was going north so I thought it would be worse to go back. We were soon through the fog and on our way to the shipping lanes. They are very busy and very intimidating the first time you see them. But you just have to keep going and when you get close to one of those big ships, go down the side of him and across his back. Be positive, then he knows that you know what you are doing. Don't try to go in front of him as he will probably be doing about 20 knots. Don't forget that good old Irish saying; be sure, to be safe.

As I got close to the ship that I had chosen to go behind I got on the radio and simply called "Big ship, big ship this is the little sailing boat on your port side in position ….". It was a great feeling when a voice came back and said "Little ship hold your course". I now felt like one of the fleet. I have always called all the ships I have ever seen, sometimes just to say good morning. I think about 95% of them have always come back and have appreciated the call. As we cleared the shipping lanes I said to David "I will have a little sleep now and you should be able to see land in about two hours". Just as I dozed off to sleep there was a massive explosion "Boom, boom". I jumped up and the first thing I said to David was "What have you done".

He said "It wasn't me, I think its that big ship over there on the horizon". I said "We must be in a firing range or something". I got on the radio but nobody came back. We carried on, not knowing what it was and you will find out later, if you haven't all ready guessed.

A few hours later we could see the big walls of Cherbourg. What a great feeling it was the first time. We were so proud of ourselves. We had a few days in Cherbourg and then made plans to go to Alderney. It was not that far away, only about twenty miles, but we left it just a little late and slightly missed the tide. You can not do that when you are going to Alderney. We were doing great and then we were sailing nicely along at about 5 knots, but Alderney was getting farther away. Yes that's right we were going backwards. The tide across the Alderney race was doing about 6.5 knots. We quickly realised what was going wrong and decided to go to Quadrille with the tide, have a swim, some lunch and then carry on to Alderney later when the tide had turned. We got to Alderney later in the day and were planning to go out for dinner. If you have been to Alderney, you will know that most people use the water taxi to and from the boats. It is a very big, black rubber dinghy. The theory is you don't get wet in it. Well, on our way in the taxi to the restaurant, a man asked when we had come across. I answered "Thursday". He said "Oh you must have had Concorde then". I did not have a clue what he was talking about. Then he said "You must have heard it going supersonic". Then we realised that was what the "Boom, boom" was that had frightened us half to death. He burst out laughing when we told him we thought someone was firing at us.

We had a good time in Alderney and then went back to Cherbourg and started to make our plans to go back. We made a plan to go back into the Solent via Bembridge and then we could say we had circumnavigated the Isle of Wight. There was no wind at all. It was like a mill pond. We started motoring, thinking the wind would pick up later. But it never did. We now had a small problem.

We had an inboard/outboard engine on 'Slipaway' and it was petrol. We had two ten litre containers and the tank was full when we left. But about halfway back I had put the second container of fuel into the tank. We had a work out of our situation and we were going to be about ten miles short of motoring all the way. We made the decision to fly the kite for three hours at three knots. This was as much time as we could sail at that speed without missing the tide. It all worked out very well for us. In fact we got to Bembridge and the dockmaster was putting us on the jetty, when, as I passed him our ropes, we ran out of petrol. That was great. We had worked it out right. But I suppose now, looking back, we either should have waited until the next day for more wind or carried more fuel. But I never expected that the English Channel could be that calm.

We carried on our holiday into the Solent for a few more weeks. Calling into Portsmouth, Chichester, Ashlett Creek and on up Southampton Water, before returning back to the Hamble. We left the boat at the Hamble and went home.

I decided that now it was time for me to do my Yachtmaster practical exam. I thought enough time had gone since I had done my Yachtmaster theory and my Day Skipper practical.

With the boat being at the Hamble, I wanted to do the exam down there because there are big tides to contend with. I felt that if I could pass in the Solent, we could sail anywhere. I made the decision to do a pre exam week with a sailing school and then book the R.Y.A examiner for the weekend. I arranged to do this with a sailing school in the Solent who were prepared to let me use my own boat. They gave me an instructor for a week. Two very good friends from the boat club in Windermere came with me as crew. We had a very hard week with the instructor.

We seemed to be on the go from early in the morning until late at night. Our instructor was a reasonably new Yachtmaster instructor but a very well-sailed gentleman. I don't think he wanted me to fail because it would not have looked good on him. I think this was the reason we were doing nearly 16 hour-days. I remember one night, we were trying to get back up the Hamble River at about

2 o'clock in the morning. I could not find the leading lights no matter how hard I tried. I just could not find it.

The instructor was a very good instructor but he was determined to make me do it myself. Eventually, about 4 o'clock in the morning, I realised that the leading light was not working and I was trying to find something that was not there. I eventually set my own bearing lines and went up the Hamble using the compass. Don't take it for granted that the lights will be working.

As the week went on, we were getting on very well together and having good fun. The instructor was a very large man and enjoyed a good laugh. We did a lot of laughing. We had a funny morning when we were on our way out of the Solent and I was on the helm. For all the world I thought that Man Island was a big ship. I kept saying "I must go to the right of this ship". In the end the instructor said to me "Can you tell me how you are going to get over that wall. That big ship you are avoiding is an island". Well you can imagine how much stick I took from the lads. I think the most memorable laugh was when the instructor was telling us about a boat he was on with a blocked toilet. He was telling us how someone had not only blocked the toilet, but had pumped the handle so much that when he undid the screws, the waste squirted everywhere and all over him. I simply said to him "Did any go in your mouth". He said "Oh yes. All over me". I replied "I thought so, it has been coming out all week". Well, we all laughed ourselves to sleep that night.

Our instructor who had become a friend by the end of the week, left us on Friday night. The R.Y.A examiner came on board on Saturday morning. Now it was all down to me to pass or fail. When the examiner got on board, I showed him through the safety equipment on the boat and asked him to try on a lifejacket and stow it somewhere where he could get it easily, if need be. I then showed him the weather forecast that I had taken down from Radio 4 that morning. He was impressed that I had made my own synopsis charts. I then asked him if he had any health problems or was he taking any medication that I should know about. I think this impressed him more than anything else. He told me he had never been asked that before. Looking back now, I think he passed me at that point. All we had to do was go out and have a good sail.

I had the best crew in my two friends that I could possibly have asked for. They did everything I asked to perfection. As a combined unit we made the exam look very easy. We had a great day out and just sailed for fun. When it was time for the examiner to go. He just said "Congratulations. I am more than happy to call you a British Yachtmaster. Your licence will come in the post from the R.Y.A". But I have to tell you, I was very fortunate to have such a good crew as my two friends; thay made it look so easy. Overall it had been a great year. But we were starting to come to the end of the season. We managed to get a few more weeks in the Solent and then brought the boat back to Windermere. We knew that sea sailing was what we really wanted to do.

Things at home were going well. The business was going well without me and I knew that next year, I would be free of it all together as I had buyers for each of the outlets. The only thing that was holding us back was the boat club as I was to be Commodore next year. I was not 100% happy with the boat, there was a lot of electronics I wanted to buy and she was getting a little old for putting that much money into her. So we decided to look for a newer boat. We were very pleased with the Hunter, so we looked at lots of different Horizons. Although they were newer than ours, they were not in as good a condition.

We had put 'Slipaway' up for sale and, to our surprise, it sold within about three weeks of going on the market. We were getting fed up of looking at bad boats and went to Southampton Boat Show to have a look at the new Hunter Ranger 265. This was a lot of boat and as I still had our trailer from 'Slipaway', which was more or less the same size, we could very easily have the trailer altered to suit the Ranger. We placed an order at the show and bought the boat in kit form. This meant it arrived as a hull full of boxes. I had to build the boat myself. This worked out quite well as it kept me busy through the winter. Whilst I was at the Boat Show, I bought a book about the Atlantic Rally for cruisers, known as the Arc, just out of interest more than anything else. I filled in a form to have information sent to us about the Arc.

We had a busy time ahead of us. We now had to build a boat, I had to be Commodore of a boat club and it was also an important time for our son, as he was about to sit his GCSE's. I also still needed some heavy weather sailing experience. I was reading more and more about heavy weather, storm techniques and reefing down, trisails and storm jibs etc. It is O.K. reading about it when you are in front of the fire, at home on a cold winters night, but I knew I needed to be out there to see what it was really like. I had more or less made all my plans for the year ahead as Commodore of the boat club. As the club had always had a very good committee, it made the job easier. I planned to be there for every function and go away on the weeks when there was nothing on, except for my holidays, when the Vice Commodore would stand in.

We started to build the new boat. We called her "Myrtle" as this was the name of the street I was born on in Liverpool. As my time at work was getting less and less I treated the project of the boat like a full time job. I would go out every morning at 7 o'clock and make a start. It was

November and they were cold mornings, but I would stop at 10am for my bacon butty and then at 1pm for my lunch, cake and tea at 3 o'clock and finish at 7pm. I did this every day up until Christmas.

We had a holiday booked on a cruise to the Caribbean which I was hoping would show us some bad weather from the safety of a big ship. After I had spoken with the Captain and shown him my Yachtmaster licence, he allowed me to go to the Bridge. This was very good because I was able to see what little yachts looked like first hand from a big ship.

It was funny how the Captain and I started talking. I was sitting at the bow of his ship with my hand held GPS, plotting our course and speed when he walked past and gave me a funny look as he said "Good morning." I just said "Good morning, don't look so worried, we are going the right way." That sort of broke the ice. He then came over and was very interested in my little GPS and also glad to see I was not planning to do anything devious to the ship. I managed to learn a lot on that ship. We covered almost two thousand five hundred miles and I spent a lot of time on the Bridge. Unfortunately, I did not get the bad weather I was hoping for. I suppose, on the other hand, because the weather was so good, this meant that Colette could sunbathe, which left me free to play with my charts. We saw a lot of sailing boats around the Caribbean and I think that is what gave me the idea to do some sunshine sailing. But I did not think, at this stage, that we would ever be contemplating crossing the Atlantic on our own boat. But I did think that we could trail our new boat, when finished, to the Mediterranean.

When we got back from holiday, I got stuck into the boat again as I wanted to finish it for the start of the next season. The project was going well and I was enjoying doing it. It is great when you can put things where you want them and know where all the wires go. I had still not had any heavy-weather sailing and I really did want to find out what it was like. So I booked to go on a Yachtmaster Instructors' course in the English Channel in February. This was to be one hundred and ten hours at sea. Let me tell you, we got bad weather. At one point we had 63 mph wind over the deck and it was so cold that my fingers and toes were burning. I was so wet and cold I felt like giving up sailing forever. All we had up was a very small trisail, and a tiny storm jib, but we were screaming along at about 8/9 knots with no visibility. The wind was blowing so hard that it constantly blew the top three foot of water off the wave into our faces. It was freezing cold. The boat we were on was only thirty two foot and was like a cork in a water-fall. As fast as we could bail it out the next wave would fill her back up. I knew we must eat, so I was going down and passing up jam on bread (jam butties). I was grabbing tins of anything and we eat them cold, straight from the tin. One of the biggest problems we had was the boom.

Although we were using a trisail which was loose footed, and the boom was fastened down by the main sheet, the boom was still right above our heads. Although it was not moving we were still being thrown onto it. In the end I had had enough of banging my head, so I lashed it down to the side rail and then our boat was a much safer place. All we had to do then was to stay in it, which was easier said than it was to do. It felt like the boat just wanted me off. I had so many bruises I could not count them. As I say I was ready to give up sailing forever.

At one stage, in the middle of the night, I rang Colette from my mobile telephone and said that I was going to pay for a helicopter to lift me off. I was quite upset and just wanted to go home. But like the iron lady she has always been she said "Don't be stupid, pull yourself together and get on with it". The next day the wind dropped down to about 40 knots and that felt quite good after the previous twenty four hours of 50-60 knots. When it dropped to 35 knots it felt great. There was another sailing boat out there that same week as us. Unfortunately, the four policemen on board all died. I think it was one of the worst weeks, weather wise, England had had for many years, but as I said I wanted some heavy weather. Now I know what it is like I hope I never have to go there again.

Looking back I learnt lots of things that week, and it's much better to do it on a school boat with four other Yachtmasters who are looking to become instructors, than it is to face it for the first time on your own boat with just you and your wife. If you are seriously thinking of going to sea, I would recommend that you book a week in bad weather as it will make a much better sailor out of you. It certainly taught me to respect the sea and its power.

When I got back I finished building "Myrtle" and we launched her in March onto Windermere. It took us seventy two, twelve hour days in total and I have to say it was very rewarding.

Well, now I was Commodore at the club and the season was going well. We were hosting the Hunter Formula One Northern Regatta. As Commodore I thought it would look good if a brand new Hunter Ranger 265 led the way as pathfinder in the first race. But guess what? With not being on the lake for a while, I was leading them all to the wrong mark. Luckily my friend was in the lead and he went the right way. As he was national champion at that time, they all followed him and not me. Once again every time you go out you should observe the six p's. *Perfect-preparation-prevents-piss-poor-performance.*

When I got back to the club I got that famous saying from someone who had just been waiting to say it. "I thought you were a Yachtmaster". Of course, I answered very nicely because, when you are doing your Masters ticket you are actually told there will be lots of people just waiting to say it. So my only answer was "Yes sir I am. But, one day, I will be as good as you and thank you for keeping an eye on me, sir".

The Ranger was very similar to the Horizon. But, with her being newer it had a lot more space and a much more open-plan form. From a sailing point of view, it was more or less the same boat, maybe with a bit more freeboard. Some people would say a bit more like a caravan, but I have to say the Ranger sails very well. We spent a little while on the lake getting to know her and then we were away to the South Coast.

This was the first time 'Myrtle' had been on the road on a long trip, as from our house to the lake was only about a five minute journey. So we weren't really sure how she would tow or perform on the road. She certainly looked very big on the trailer, as you can see from the photo. I thought it would be best if we had our annual lads week first. This way we could get the mast up with ease.

We left early Saturday morning so as to miss the traffic out of Windermere and onto the motorway. With the six wheel trailer and the stabiliser she was towing like a dream. But we knew that we were right on the British towing limits for length, width and weight. It did look very big. We were dreading seeing a police car. Well we nearly made it. We had just come off the motorway onto the A34, when, the next thing, there was a police car right up my back.

He started to flash me and pulled us over. When we stopped he said we were too big and over weight. I said "Do you mean me or the boat". But he did not see the funny side. I knew then that this guy was going to be hard work.

He got on his radio and told someone he wanted the weigh-bridge about three miles down the road opening up. He told us to follow him. Well at least with this policeman we were going to find out whether we were legal or not. We got to the weigh-bridge and another person turned up to open it. Onto the weigh-bridge we went. After a load of messing about they finally had it all switched on and ready to weigh us.

The policeman was not very happy to find that we were absolutely bang on the limit. You can imagine his face. He then proceeded to measure our length. Again, unfortunately for him, we were within the limit. He then went on to measure our width, but I knew from our gateposts at home that, when we took the boat out through the gateposts we had a quarter of an inch either side to spare. So, we were actually half an inch within the legal limit.

Now our policeman was not very happy and he was starting to get very bad-tempered. In his anger he went of to the back of the boat and starting checking our brand new light board, which was actually working to perfection. His next move was to check the straps holding the boat onto the trailer. We had eight brand new three inch wide wagon-ratchet straps. He was so determined to find something wrong I actually started to feel sorry for him. He started checking our tyres. I had just fitted six brand new low profile reinforced Michelin tyres onto the trailer and four brand new Goodyears onto the Discovery. He then came out with that classic line "I'll let you go this time". I just said "Thank you very much sir". We drove away as they locked up the weigh-bridge. Well at least he got to lock something up.

It was quite good for us really because we had a complete, free road test, and we probably couldn't have found a more nasty person to do it. But we kept our sense of humour and our spirits high and carried on down the road to the River Hamble. Because we had been detained for an hour or two, with our policeman friend, we were a bit later than we wanted to be arriving at the Hamble and unfortunately missed the travel hoist service. We decided that, rather than wait until the next day, we would slip the boat in ourselves from the trailer. We put the mast up on the trailer, as this was much easier to do, and then attached a long rope and slipped the whole thing into the water. It worked very well. It was low water, so I knew that even if it had gone wrong it would have floated off the trailer anyway, at high water.

The next day we were off to Cowes and the day after to Lymington. From there, we made our plans to go to

Alderney. I don't think I have told you yet that at this stage in my sailing life, I suffered very badly from sea-sickness. In fact, virtually every time I went to sea. I would have to take lots of tablets. If you are the same as me, don't worry 70 - 80% of people that start sailing are the same. I had tried all kinds of different things. I found that Slimline Tonic was very good. If you open the can and drink it very fast, its so gassy that it makes you burp, and I believe that this helps the food go to the bottom of your stomach instead of floating around. Well that's my theory. Other people say that Tonic is good because it has quinine in it, that also could be true. People say that Coca Cola is very good because it has caffeine in it. But I think that common sense is one of the best treatments for sea-sickness. Light, dry snacks before you sail are very good. Ginger is also very good for sea sickness, so ginger biscuits work very well. So, there is a snack in itself, ginger biscuits and Coca Cola.

But as usual, the night before we left for Alderney, lads being lads, we had our fair share of bitter, garlic prawns, steak and chips, apple pie and cream and our night cap of Stilton cheese and a wee drop of whisky. We then left at 4 o'clock in the morning for Alderney. One of the lads gave me a large Mars bar and a pint of milk. Well, no prizes for guessing who Christened 'Myrtle' first.

We decided to go to Cherbourg first. We had a very

good crossing and it was quite funny when I just happened to see the white arrow in the sky.

Yes, this time I knew what it was. But the other lads didn't know what was coming next. I asked one of them to check if the battery was O.K. in the aft locker, and just as he got to the battery container the next thing was "Boom, boom". As they jumped out of their skin, I just said "Oh, there's Concorde". I must say it is an unbelievable sound and, even though you know it's about to happen, it still gives you a fright.

We had a good laugh the next morning in France, just sitting in the street, drinking fresh coffee and eating ham baguettes in one of the small cafes, watching as all the people were going to start their working day. We were trying to work out the Continental kissing system. To this day I still don't understand it.

There was a particularly interesting guy we were watching. He was a very smart gentleman, about thirty years of age, with a very classy Armani suit and a nice pair of leather shoes. He was obviously the owner of one of the stores and he seemed to know every lady in France. Some of the ladies would come over to him to say good morning and he would kiss them twice, once on each cheek. We worked it out that two kisses meant just an acquaintance. Then, he would kiss some of the ladies three times. We think that they must have been good friends. Then, he would kiss some ladies four times. We reckon that they must have been very good friends. Then, to our surprise, he kissed a really beautiful lady five times. You don't want to know what we worked out that meant! Anyway, as they say, small things amuse small minds.

We moved on the next day to Alderney. This was a very interesting little passage: something happened that had never happened to me before, and has actually only ever happened to me once since. They say that you normally only get fog when there is no wind. Well, I can tell you now that is not true. It was a very nice morning and we were sailing nicely across the coast of France at about 5 knots. The wind conditions were great, about 15-18 knots from the north east. So that was ideal for us, but the wind started to increase, so we began to reef down a little bit. The wind was picking up to about 25 knots, with little gusts of 28-30 off the end of the island. This was quite pleasant for us four lads who enjoyed sailing. All of a sudden, in from behind us, came a fog bank. Now I know this sounds a bit strange, to have fog in 25 knots of wind, but there we were, sails up, doing 6 knots, the wind blowing and we couldn't see a thing. The fog bank was so thick that it was hard to see the front of the boat. We started to take down the sails. We had all put on our harnesses and clip lines, obviously, as I am sure you would do. Then, this damn great fog horn at the end of Alderney was howling at us. This was our first proper experience of fog. I had only ever had a little bit, once before, going over the Channel, but that didn't last very long. This time we were in a real fog bank. The wind decreased to about 15 knots as we approached Alderney then, suddenly, the wind seemed to stop. We were stuck right in the centre of what seemed to be a huge ball of fog. Now that we had all the sails safely stored away we were moving along very slowly over the water, with the engine on. Unfortunately the water was running over the ground at about 5 knots, so Alderney was fast approaching at about 7 knots.

For those of you who don't know the approaches to the Channel Islands, they are strewn with rocks and Alderney is notorious for boats running aground. As we couldn't see a thing, these rocks were playing on my mind, and that damn great fog horn wasn't helping: it seemed to be getting closer and closer. It is a horrible thing to sail in fog as you can't help but think that any minute now, a big black thing is going to appear and run you down. All onboard were very, very quiet and that eerie feeling certainly plays games with your mind.

As on most boats nowadays, we had a G.P.S. on board so we were able to do an accurate fix every ten minutes. The G.P.S. that I had fitted was a plotter, so, not only did it give us a fix, but it also showed us a chart of exactly where we were. This took away a lot of the anxiety with the chart work. I am a great believer in paper charts and, on normal passages, it is the norm for us to put down a G.P.S. and fix onto the chart every thirty minutes. Some people may say that this is too much, but I believe that by writing down your position every thirty minutes on your log sheet, your crew become very competent at being able to do a fix and, if ever we get into a distress situation, at least my crew and I would always know our position within two or three miles.

We also believe that it is a great advantage to be checking things like water temperature, oil pressure etc. when the engine is running. My friends and I have always said that the plotter that we fitted onto 'Myrtle' paid for itself that particular day when we went into Alderney because, in the end, the fog was so bad I went downstairs, watched the plotter, and gave instructions to my friend who was on the helm. Very simply; go left, go right and we steered our way using the plotter and the depth sounder all the way into Bray Harbour. We actually managed to pick up a mooring buoy without being able to see anything else in the harbour. I think we were just very lucky that we never ran into any other moored or anchored vessels. It was only a few hours later, when the fog lifted, that we actually got to see Alderney.

The plotter that we had at that time was the most up to date that there was. New plotters now have a Radar unit built in. Plotters are great for letting you know where you are, but are fantastic in fog when you can see where the boats are on your radar. We spent the next few days in Alderney as the weather started getting worse. It was blowing 35 knots in the harbour and it was very uncomfortable on the mooring. We had our boom out over to one side and had a bucket hanging into the water. This made it a bit better, but it was still very uncomfortable.

We went for a walk the next day just to get off the boat. We walked up to the airport to have a look at the small aircraft that go from island to island. This is where I caught my crew pricing flights back to England. But they never went; they decided to sail back with me instead. The forecast was getting worse for the weekend and nobody was very happy on the boat just rocking and rolling all day and all night. We got up the next day and it was blowing about 25-28 knots from the south. So I made the decision to go back to the Solent. We left at 9 o'clock in the morning. The forecast was for force 7/8 later. I thought that it would take us about twelve hours to get back. But we had a flier and were at the Needles in eight and a half hours. The little problem we had now was that the tide was still coming out of the Solent at about 3 knots.

As the wind was from the south, it was causing a big

sea but, as the wind was blowing harder, we were going faster and ploughing our way into the Solent like a train. In no time at all we were up in Yarmouth having our steak and chips. This was a great test for 'Myrtle' and we were very happy with her performance. We left the boat at Hamble Point Marina and went back to Windermere.

Because of my commitment as Commodore at the club we weren't able to get to the boat as much as we wanted. But this also fitted in well with our son's GCSE exams; so Colette was able to be at home to push him. We did manage to get to the Solent a few weeks later. We left on Sunday after the club had closed and went back the following Friday before it opened.

Although this was only a four day sailing trip it was good. We just went up to Chichester and that was very exciting. On the way back the forecast was for a SE 3-4. But when we got to the Chichester Bar it was actually blowing 35 knots and the swell was putting 'Myrtle' to the test. We had a VHF speaker outside in the cockpit and Colette was holding onto the handrail next to the stair-well, but her ear was right next to the speaker from which two Maydays were being called.

There was a French boat that had been blown onto the Bramble Bank and there was also another boat that was sinking. We were being tossed about like a cork but, when we got behind the shelter of the Isle of Wight, it was not too bad for us. When we finally got back up the River Hamble there were a lot of complaints about the morning forecast. However, you must remember that forecasts are just that.

Whilst away that week, we decided that once David had finished his exams we would go to Spain for a few weeks. We made some enquiries, found out all the ferry times and decided to take the boat to the Mediterranean on the ferry.

We were mid way into the season at the club and, as it was near the end of June, we were looking forward to our trip to the Mediterranean. We left on Sunday, again after the club had closed, and the Vice Commodore was going to stand in for me for the next two weeks. We arrived down at the boat later that evening and David had brought a friend from school with him. This made it very easy for us to get the mast down. We spent all day Monday making sure that we had everything right on the boat. As our ferry would take us from Southampton to Bilbao we then had to drive to Alicante, which was about six hundred miles. So, we did not want anything to go wrong with the boat or trailer. We were hoping to be towing at 60 m.p.h. but that was not possible a lot of the way, because we had to drive over some very steep hills. At times our speed was down to 20 m.p.h. We actually made it to Alicante at

11 o'clock at night, so we were on the road just about fifteen hours. Our average speed was about 40 m.p.h. I think this was about the best speed we could have made as we had no hold ups; there were just some very steep hills.

The next day, we drove down to El Campello Marina. This was a very new marina and the staff were very helpful and efficient. You know they say to leave everything to the professionals; well I didn't. I was interfering while the men in the yard were trying to put the boat in the water. They had a funny looking thing, it was like a big fork lift truck, with a big square iron frame and two straps that went around the boat. I jumped up on the boat and said that famous saying "You don't do it like that, you do it like this". As I said it I turned around and walked straight into the big iron frame with my head. As I looked down, David, his friend and the two Spanish workmen were laughing their heads off. We were back to laughter, but I tell you what, my head didn't half hurt! After that I left the men to get on with it, kept my mouth shut and they did a great job, taking care with the boat all the way.

It didn't take us long to get the mast up and rigged. We were getting quite good at it by now. So here we were sailing the Mediterranean. Our first trip was from El Campello to Alicante, which has a very large harbour.

Once you round the wall at the entrance, you then have

about two miles to go up through the docks to get to the marina, which is right in the middle of the city. And what a fantastic city it is.

We did not think that we would see boats as big as the ones in Alicante. But, then again, we never thought we would sail across the Atlantic. We very quickly started to learn that sailing in the Med is totally different to sailing in England, Ireland or Scotland. You must start to think about dangers that you don't normally think of. But, as you continue to read on, you will say that these are all common sense and yes, they are, now that we have written them all down.

The first is the risk of sunburn, not just for you, but also for the other people on board. Make sure you have plenty of different strengths of sun cream on the boat. Leave them in obvious places, so that people are tempted to put the stuff on. Make sure that they are being used. It is your responsibility as a skipper. It is much easier to work with a crew that are fit and healthy than it is to work with people who are moaning every time they move. We once had a person on board who was very dark-haired and skinned; we thought he could take the sun quite well. He had never had a problem before with sunburn and he thought that he could take the sun too. What he didn't realise was that because we were sailing along in a bit of wind with a nice breeze coming over the deck, the sun

SEA YE LATER

PETER

WHY NOT

COLETTE

SLIPAWAY

ME

Ciao Moody

POLY MER

EL CAMPELLO

BOBBY

MINNIE HA HA

was burning him up. In the middle of the night we got a knock on our cabin door. This person was in a lot of pain. We tried our best to cool him down but he was running a high temperature. We tried calamine lotion and wet, cold pads to try and soothe his burning back. When he went to hospital a few days later, the whole of his back had become blistered and septic and they said that he was suffering from third degree burns!! So please bear in mind that the sun is very hot. At the end of the day, your crew's health will become your problem, whether you like it or not.

The next danger is that food goes off very fast in the heat. At this point, we did not have a fridge on 'Myrtle'. You should seriously consider buying one before you take your boat to the Med or any other hot country. We had a cool box on 'Myrtle', which was about as much use as an ashtray on a motorbike. The milk would turn within hours of being opened, any cooked meats would start to sweat and, because the cool box would heat up so fast, it was only good as a breeding ground for germs. The last thing you want is a crew with dickie tummies. Once one person gets it, you can pretty much guarantee that someone else will get it within days. Plenty of plastic storage containers are very useful. Screw down or seal down type of lids are best. Try to use as much storage space below the water line as you can. At least it stays relatively cool down there.

We found that vacuum packed meats lasted a few days longer than ordinary wrapped meats.

The next is the water and your water tank. Because you are constantly warming the water by day and cooling it by night, it becomes a great environment for germs. Make sure you use plenty of sterilising tablets. Put them into the water tank and fit filters into the line if you can. If you are in a marina where there is a supply of good clean water, every so often rinse your lines out with a bit of biocide or a solution of bleach to keep the lines fresh and clear. We tend to use our tank water for washing and cleaning and for boiling. Always keep a good supply of bottled water for normal daily drinking.

The next danger is the dreaded mosquitos. You will be eaten alive if you don't do something about them. You need to make or buy nets for your windows and hatches. Make sure you have plenty of mosquito repellent on board. We have these small electric devices that you put a tablet into and we find that if we leave a couple of these plugged in when we are in marinas, they tend to kill off any mosquitos that get on board. The other thing we do quite often is, that when we go out for the day, we spray each cabin before we leave and then lock all the boat up, including the hatches and windows. There is nothing worse than when you are making a small passage, coming off your watch, trying to sleep and a mosquito wants you for his dinner.

The problem is that you can try sleeping with the sheet over your head, but then you start to overheat, so in the end you have to get up to try to find the culprit. But mosquitos are too clever. I don't know where they hide, but as soon as you switch the light off and try to go back to sleep, out they come again for their dessert. What happens is that when you do eventually find him, it is your turn to go back on watch!

Please don't be put off the Mediterranean by these little things, just make sure you do something about them before you get there. The Mediterranean is a wonderful place to sail. You can sail as far or as near as you want because there are very good marinas every ten or twenty miles. Sometimes the next marina is only four miles away. The marina rates are very low compared to anywhere else we have sailed. They are about 75% less that the Solent and 50% less that Scotland and Ireland. Sometimes we wish we were back there as we miss that good old Spanish hospitality that you find in all the Tapas bars, the Spanish sense of humour and the low, low prices. You can see why there are boats that never leave the Mediterranean.

We left Alicante, as we had David and his friend with us and they wanted to see Benidorm (a crazy place), where the youngsters can drink and dance all night and sleep it off all the next day on the beach. Oh, to be 18 again, eh?

The marina at Benidorm is not very big; well, it wasn't when we were last there. But things in Spain move very fast. What one day would be a field could, within months, could be a theme park. What you might find one year as a small anchorage or a small marina, the next year could be a multi-million pound complex. The Spanish certainly seem to be very good at re-development.

There are marinas either side of Benidorm; There is Villajoyasa on one side and Altea on the other. If you want a night out that won't stop, Benidorm is the place, not exactly our cup of tea, but David and his friend loved it. The beauty of this part of Spain is that you can go mad in Benidorm or sail two hours up the coast and be sitting in a little fishing harbour in total peace and quiet. There is so much to do. I know now why some people never leave the Mediterranean. You can have fun in the sun for nine months of the year *and* low cost sailing. There are lots of marinas offering good winter storage rates. After we had the week-end in Benidorm we decided to go west again, pass Alicante and go to the Isle of Tabarca. We have been laughing about one of the stories from that trip ever since.

What happened was, we had some friends who lived in El Campello, who we had seen a few times during our stay there that week. They had a small speed boat. As we were going along, Colette needed to go to the toilet. I saw a small boat coming up behind me quite fast. As we were a few miles off shore I was a little bit concerned. It was approaching us very fast. I quickly realised it was our friends from El Campello. Just as they got to the back of the boat, Colette came up from down below. She said "Oh hi. I didn't know you were there, I was just in the loo". They said "Yes. We know it's just gone past us". I won't tell you what Colette said but it started with "I can't even**** in peace". Oh boy, did we laugh.

We had a good day over in Tabarca and were anchored just off the island. There was no marina there. It was a reasonably quiet day without a lot of wind. The anchor was down and holding well. I was just a little bit apprehensive about some of the cloud patterns in the sky. Don't get me wrong, I am not the best at reading the weather from the sky, but I know when I have a gut feeling. There were some funny colours, not something I had ever seen before, there was a forecast for rain. I watched the sky for a while and then went on to that other saying of mine "If in doubt get out". We decided to go to Santa Pola, which was only about fifteen miles back across to the mainland. We were so glad that we made the decision to go as, that night, we had never seen thunder and lightning like it in our lives. The rain was so bad that it was running down the street about twelve inches deep. It was unbelievable. We were sitting in a restaurant watching chairs go floating past the window. We were so very pleased that we were not sitting on that anchorage. You do get a fair old share of rain in the Med. but what I used to do was to quickly take all my clothes off, grab the shampoo and make the most of it. It's not like the U.K. where you would have to get all your wet weather gear on (as it would probably be cold and last for about 4 days).

The rain in the Med. is warm, usually only lasts for about twenty minutes and then the sun comes back out and dries everything back up. After Santa Pola, we then went on to San Juan and then back to Alicante. We left the boat there for one month. The security at Alicante is excellent. They have video cameras all over the marina, even a video on the water entrance to the marina. There are security men in a control office that are watching about ten screens, twenty four hours a day throughout the whole marina. So, don't go for a sly pee over the side unless you don't mind spaniards laughing at your little fella!

The marina is only about fifteen minutes from the airport and is therefore an ideal place to leave your boat. The young ladies in the office are extremely helpful and go out of their way to welcome you. I think that this is one of the advantages of having so many marinas so close together; the competition between them is quite healthy. If people are not happy or the rates are too high, they simply move on to the next marina.

It is amazing how quickly the time is now flying by. It is mid June 1997, and soon my responsibilities at the boat club would be coming to an end as, at the L.D.B.C you are only Commodore for one season. I think this is a good idea as it keeps new people moving through the club and new ideas coming up all the time. It is like everything else, if you let it go stale, it is hard to swallow.

I was not able to get back out to the boat then for about a month as it was a busy time at the club. As it was the height of the season, we had a lot of different functions on. Although I was not able to get out to the boat, this was giving me more time to do more and more reading. I was receiving magazines from the World Cruising Club and finding reading about the Arc extremely interesting; admiring those people.

Now at that time I thought that the type of people who were sailing across the Atlantic were real hardened sailors with years and years of experience. Even at this stage I still had no ambition to cross the Atlantic. In fact, to be quite honest with you, the thought of 40 - 50 knots of wind and 10 -15 metre seas and hurricanes popping up all over the place frightened me to death. Although I did admire the people that were doing it, especially when I read about some people who were doing it who were in their 70's and 80's!!

At home, people would ask us about our sailing adventures and what we were doing next. We told people that we would love to sail to Gibraltar. I don't know why Gibraltar but it seemed to be one of the next challenges on our list. There were also the Balearic Islands, Ibiza, Minorca, Majorca etc. It seemed that every time we spoke with a different person we would hear about a different place. It is funny but the more you talk, the more you want to go there.

David got his GCSE exam results. This was a very anxious time for us as David was our priority. He got 3 A+'s, 6 A's and 1 B. He was not very happy about the B, but, as I said to him, you can't get it all right all of the time. Look at me I make mistakes virtually every time I go sailing. This is the way we learn. Colette and I were extremely pleased with his results. I know that behind our backs people thought that we were leaving David on his own too much but now the results were speaking for themselves and David was very happy to have time on his own for a week or for a long weekend as he would have his friends round at the house. After all, our house is his house and we have no restrictions on who he can have there. He was very happy even the first time we left him for two weeks. What people didn't realise was there was never a day when we didn't speak to him on the telephone or one of mine or Colette's family would be with him.

I know what it is like to be left alone; it happened to me when I was only nine, so I know how important it is to make sure that your kids are happy and secure, if you can. Unfortunately, my mother never got the chance. David was now starting his A levels and I didn't think he would be coming sailing for a while. But he did not want us to stop sailing.

We went back to the boat with two friends from the boat club. I had been away a few times on lads' weeks with the men but had never been away before with a lady. As we had not been away with them before we decided just to have a week. That way, if we were getting on each others nerves, a week is not too long. We sailed down to Mar Menor. This is an inland sea and a great place to have a good holiday. There are lots of things to do and we were getting on very well together. All wished that we had booked two weeks as one week flew by very fast. We called in at Torrevijeca on our way up to El Campello and then on back to Alicante. My friend likes to get into the heart of the place. I mean the real heart; the real dives, the back streets and to meet the real locals. This is not 100% what Colette enjoys but, if you invite people to your boat, you must be prepared to give and take. I am sure that if you don't, you will all fall out. You must also be prepared to bite your lip sometimes because two ladies in a kitchen, two men in an engine room and four people in a small space is a recipe for arguments, unless you are a good skipper. Be prepared to go your own way somedays and let your friends have days on their own. What we tend to do is go out together in the morning, then split up and go our own way and meet up again later, rather than trying to do everything together. You must talk openly and decide before you go what each likes and dislikes. If your friends want to go out one night on their own or you want to go to a different place than them, be open about it and do it. Set out the boat rules before you start the holiday. That way you will have a happy ship and a longer lasting friendship.

We still have a good laugh about the last day of that holiday. We were on the quay at Alicante when, all of a sudden, the biggest pair of masts we had ever seen came around the corner. They were all white with polished stainless steel fittings. The whole boat was white. It glistened in the sun. It was millions of pounds worth. As it came alongside, all of the crew were dressed in white uniforms. Even the fenders were polished. There was a big set of hydraulic steps that came out of the side and yes, of course, they were white with polished stainless steel rails. The only thing on the boat that was a different colour was a beautiful young lady, sitting on deck right at the front of the boat, all dressed in black. We were very intrigued by the whole thing. It was like something from a film. I sometimes think the lady was the definition of class but the skipper was a first class pratt. As we were sitting eating our garlic prawns and having our small glass of Cervesa outside the restaurant next door to the office, he came over to check in, but the office was closed for siesta. He asked us what time the office opened. I told him and asked him where he had sailed from. He replied "Puerto Banus." I said "We have been down to Mar Menor, have you been there?". He replied "And what would we want to go there for". Pratt!!

The holiday we had with our two friends went very well and we wouldn't hesitate to ask them to come with us again. I know that Colette and I have some funny ways, but tell me, who doesn't? But at least there are two friends who are able to put up with us and we find them very good company. In fact Colette and the lady never shut up; they seem to be able to talk day and night, non-stop. I think they could talk forever and not get fed up.

One of the things that we found we were doing more and more in the Mediterranean was stopping for a lunch time swim. I think this was because it was so hot. So, we found we were laying the anchor most days. Now all those hours and hours of anchor-practice that we had done on Windermere were paying off. You know how some people just drop a load of anchor and chain over the side? you can't get away with that in the Mediterranean. There are not that many anchorages so, what there are, are normally very busy. So you must learn to drop an anchor so that it lands, then drop the boat back slowly and pay the chain out so that the hook takes. Don't just drop a load of chain in a big pile at the bottom.

I remember once there was a day when we were out on Windermere practising anchoring. We would lay the anchor, then pick it up, then relay it, up and down most of the day. But by the end of the day we were getting a bit fed up working with the anchor. It was time to have some tea so we decided to pick up a mooring buoy. Colette said "There's one over there to the right". I said "You want me to go to the right" because I could not see a mooring buoy. "Go right" she said "There's one there". So in the end I went right. David and I could see what she was looking at but we just played along. Colette was adamant she could see a mooring buoy. But we knew she was wrong. But you just couldn't tell her. Anyway, in the end she got the boat hook ready to pick up her so-called mooring buoy. But the swan just flew away!!!

Now if you think that's bad Colette once went into a butchers shop in St. Helens and asked if her glasses were ready. The man behind the counter said "I think you want the opticians next door, love". People sometimes wonder why I operate a two man watch with Colette. It is a good job that she is so good at everything else on the boat. I do think that she would be my best crew member even if she didn't have her glasses.

A month later, we managed to get out again for another week. We just went up and down the coast, just finding new places and meeting lots of new friends. You tend to see the same boats, as the cruising community is quite big. You know how it is; you come in, another boat will help you with your lines and you start talking to them. They normally ask you onboard for a drink, you ask them onboard your boat for a drink, so you are never really on your own, unless you choose to be. This is the really nice thing about cruising. Everyone you meet is doing the same thing, all having the same conversation and there is always someone there to help if you have a problem.

We had a problem, this time out, when we were at Altea. You know how it is, you spend all your time thinking about safety on a boat and I think you are always a bit cautious when you are on land in a foreign country. Well, I am anyway, especially after being brought up in Liverpool city centre. It does make you a little bit street wise.

The last place on earth I would have thought we would have had a problem was at an outdoor church festival. There was a large gathering of people on the promenade walkway. It was the local church at Altea, having a festival. There were lots of lovely people and Colette and I decided to watch. The whole thing was taking place on the beach. All the children were dressed in their Sunday best. It was a lovely atmosphere. Colette was sitting on the steps to the beach and I was standing just in front of her. There were lots of people behind us. As the play was going on there were pyrotechnics (O.K. fireworks). All of a sudden there was an almighty explosion about fifty yards in front of us. It was one of the loudest things we had ever heard. One of the very big fireworks had exploded sidewards in the metal canister and the canister had gone off like a bomb. The shrapnel went everywhere. When I lifted my head, Colette was lying flat on her back and blood was pouring from her mouth. She had been hit in the face by the bottom of the canister. We could not work out at first what had happened. There were people everywhere with blood pouring from their legs, heads, faces and arms. There was one man right next to us with blood pumping from his leg. A piece of the canister had cut his main artery.

I quickly covered Colette's face as I did not want blood from anyone else going on her. She was very frightened and did not know what had happened and, of course, could not see how bad the cut was. I was trying to assure her that it was not that bad. But when you have a lot of blood running from your mouth, you can imagine how scared you are. There were lots and lots of people screaming and some Spanish ladies came over to help us. I know they were only trying to help, but were actually making matters worse by wailing and apologising to us. They were crying things like "Oh the poor lady's face" and other things in Spanish. You can imagine Colette thought her head was hanging off. We eventually made our way into the ambulance and I kept Colette's face covered. I think this was the first time I had managed to shut Colette up. We were put in the same ambulance as the man with the cut artery and there was a lot of blood around.

The red cross were very good and got us to the hospital. When we eventually managed to get rid of all the wailing women from the hospital, the doctor had a look at

Colette's mouth and patched her up. Thankfully, it was not too bad and looked worse than it actually was. We were very lucky.

We went back the next day to work out what had happened with the police. I had the piece of canister that had hit Colette. It was the base of the tube. Colette also had a round cut on the inside of her knee. When she sat back in the same place where she was sitting on the step, we could see exactly what had happened. There was a large piece of concrete step missing between her legs. The disc had hit the step, ricocheted off, hit her leg and had then shot up to her mouth. She was very lucky; I think if the disc had been a fraction higher it would have gone right through her. When we got back to the boat she was comforted by some lovely people from other boats and, thankfully, all was well. I will never know, to this day, how it missed me as I was standing directly in front of Colette. I suppose it just wasn't my turn. Despite the accident, we still had a great holiday and managed to get a few more sails in before the end of that year. We finally had the boat lifted out at Lois Campomaris or Greenwich as it is sometimes known; it's longitude is 00 00.

We went home for the winter and had our annual laying-up dinner at the club. This meant that my year as Commodore was basically over. Although I was Commodore until March the club was closed so there was not a lot I had to do.

We went to the Boat Show. This time with two friends who we had been away sailing with earlier in the year. While we were at the show, my friend asked if I would let him buy half of 'Myrtle'. This seemed like a good idea, as we all got on very well. We were not using the boat every week, as we still had David to consider and his A levels were very important. We had a proper legal document drawn up, so that there would be no misunderstanding in the future.

I think that if you get it right from the start and put in your contract what you are thinking and wanting, a boat share is a very good thing. You only have to pay half the running costs etc. In our agreement we arranged that we would take the boat to the Balearic Islands for one year and then on to Croatia, for two years. There were lots of other do's and don'ts in our contract. Eventually we were both happy with our document, so it was signed, sent to the small ships register and we legally transferred 32 of the 64 boat shares to our friends. I don't know why a boat is divided into 64 boat shares, I can only think it is because this number divides easily to provide for multi shareholding. With this new agreement now in place, we were raring to go and could not wait for March to come around so that we could sail to the Balearic Islands.

As I said earlier in this book, I have done a lot of strange things in my life, but looking back, I am surprised myself, that I did the next one. Believe it or not, I booked for a week in the Solent again on 1st February '98 for heavy weather sailing. I had learnt that much the year before, that this time I was well prepared. I had bought myself the best pair of sailing boots I could find. I had thermal underwear on every day and the best pair of Goretex gloves there was. I had a Goretex sailing balaclava and a full ski-suit that I used as pyjamas. I was determined not to get cold. I had a very good weekend, and enjoyed every minute of it. We had winds of about 35-40 knots but that was enough to remind me of the seas power. Whilst I was away that week, there was a delivery skipper on the same course and I had a good few conversations with him. He had done a lot of Atlantic crossings and he really wasn't much better than me. I think this is what started me thinking about the Atlantic. Some of the things he was telling me about some of the people that crossed the Atlantic, made me start to feel quite confident that Colette and I could do this. Although this man started me thinking, I myself thought that I still was not ready. To be honest, the thought of being at sea for twent five to thirty days quietly frightened me. But when people talk about it, it was very hard not to get involved, it is easy to say "Maybe one day" though. Deep down I never thought that we would actually do it.

We still had enough to get on with, with 'Myrtle' and our new partnership. We again, as usual, had the first week of the season as a lads' week. We flew out to Lois Campomaris to take the boat across to the Balearic Islands. We had taken our hired liferaft back to the U.K. at the end of the last season, as its hire period had run out. We decided to buy a new one. We bought the new raft from a company in Spain, as you are not allowed to transport life-rafts on an aircraft. The one that I bought was a four man, valise-type, fully automatic offshore raft. It sounds a bit over the top for a twenty seven foot boat, but I reckon whether it is twenty seven foot or one hundred and seven foot, it would be nice to have something to step into if you had to get off. Owing to the fact that 'Myrtle' was making sixty to one hundred mile passages I thought it was a good investment. The valise type looks like a holdall and is very easy to stow away and keep dry. The canister type are the ones that you see strapped on decks or, normally, on the back rail. The one that I bought for 'Myrtle' stores nicely in the forward berth, at the side, standing up and could be easily got at, if needed. I know that life rafts are a lot of money and you can hire them, but if the boat is going to be in the water for nine months, it is cheaper to buy one than to hire. It is like all safety equipment; it is a lot of money for something that you never want to use. But the day that they save your life they are very cheap.

We went up the coast to Javia first and then onto Calpi. The marina there sits in the bay at Calpi Rock and this is the nearest point to the Balearics; to Formentera, anyway.

In our normal fashion, we went into town the night before we left and had too much to eat and a bit to drink. I don't know why we do it, but all boat owners seem to be the same. We left at about 4 o'clock in the morning for Formentera, which is about seventy miles away. I reckoned on about fourteen hours, which would get us in while it was still light. If I can, I always try to get into a marina or anchorage that I am visiting for the first time, before dark. We were about three hours into the passage when all of a sudden, a six foot green thing came rushing across the cockpit, from downstairs, in the nude. Yes, one of the crew had eaten too many garlic prawns. About one hour later, I started, then somebody else, and then we were all quite bad all the way across. We had a very wallowy passage and the wind was slightly on the nose. We were having to bear away quite a bit.

We motor-sailed most of the way and eventually

arrived about 5 o'clock. I felt like I could happily have left the boat there for ever. I did not feel like going on the next day to Ibiza, but it is like falling off a bike; you have to get back on the next day and get on with it.

Lonely poem.

When you are on the waves
    away from land
    No, you can't see the bottom,
    No, you can't see the sand,

Occasionally the odd bird flies by
    And seems to say hello,
    But then you are back on your own
    because they quickly go,

Your mind tends to wander into the night
    I don't know whether it's fear,
    apprehension or just good old fright.

I keep hoping that one morning I will meet
    with the big cruise ships,
    I will ask on the radio
    What are the chances of
    A big steak and chips?

It is funny how your mind works
    When there is nothing else to do,
    And that's why I wrote the book

It's funny but it's true.

I went to the Pharmacia (chemist) when we got ashore and bought some sea sickness tablets. The ones I bought were called Cinfamar Caffina. I found that they worked very well for me. For the first time, I found sea sickness tablets that kept me awake instead of making me tired. It is because of the caffeine. We have since found that the tablets were made of anti-histamine and caffeine. So, now we buy Nitol and Pro Plus which are basically the same thing. Well they definitely work for Colette and I.

The next day we bashed on to Ibiza and Majorca and finally ended up in Arenal (Little Germany). We left the boat there and went home. At the end of the week, and not for the first time, we had had yet another successful week. It was full of good fun and laughter. One of the things that I like about going away for a week with the lads, is what you always learn from other people. Even if it is only a little thing, it still makes you a better sailor. The other thing is, I think that old saying "Absence makes the heart grow fonder" is definitely true. After two or three days I always want to go home to Colette. I miss her so much.

As the new Commodore had taken over at the boat club and I was now free to go away whenever I wanted, we decided that we would try leaving our son a little bit longer each time we went away, and go away for two weeks at a time. Our next trip was in April back to Arenal, then to Palma Bay and Puerto Nous. The Balearics are a very nice sailing area with lots of bays and marinas and, if you want, you can day-sail between the islands. You have to be a little bit careful as the wind tends to get up in the afternoon and can blow quite hard at times. So, make sure you practice reefing down as the wind tends to come very fast. 1998 was a very good sailing year for us. We managed to sail all over the Balearics and covered over fifty marinas and bays.

I had another trip in the same year. A friend of mine was going to sail in the Cork Week Regatta. He asked me if I would sail his boat from Inverkip in Scotland to Crosshaven in Ireland. At the time I was seriously considering asking Colette to consider doing the Arc in year 2000. I thought that this trip would help me make my decision. This was probably going to be my longest trip to date. I agreed to do the trip in the May of that year. A few days before we left I had butterflies in my stomach. The thought of the notorious Irish Sea was frightening me a little bit as was knowing that my friends and others at home would be watching for my every mistake. The owner of the boat gave me a free hand to buy all the charts and pilots I wanted. So, if I got it wrong now, there was definitely no one else to blame. I thank my friend for that opportunity because, at that time, not even Colette knew that I was thinking of crossing the Atlantic Ocean. We left Inverkip at around 8 o'clock that night and headed first for Bangor, Northern Ireland. By 8 o'clock the next morning, we were in thick fog. Now the test was on.

I did not have a chart plotter on board this time and no radar. But we did have a GPS. So, I decided that we would draw grids on the chart and would sail from grid to grid. We then made the decision to sail past Bangor and stay out because the fog was so bad. It lasted about 24 hours in all. We made our first landfall in Ardglass about half way down. One of the things we did have on board was a fold away radar deflector, which we had hoisted on the rigging. We had a near miss as we were passing Bangor. It was a ferry that shot straight across the front of us, within about one hundred yards. I called him on the radio and asked the Captain if he could see us. He replied that he could see us on his radar. I asked why he had came so close, and he replied there was no problem. I told him that we had the kettle on, and that he had thrown the boat all over the place and perhaps I should report the incident to the coast guard. Then, and only then, did we get an apology from the Captain, and rightly so. I am glad we had our radar deflector up. You would be surprised how strong they appear on a radar screen. I now have a tubular radar deflector on my backstay and also a big radar bleeper half way up the mast. You know the type they look like a fender. I can tell you after being on the bridge of some very big ships, that the yachts that have deflectors on show up much clearer on the radar than the ones that don't.

This was the only mishap we had on the trip and we got to Crosshaven about four days later. Because of the very strong tides in the Irish Sea, you must make sure you do your preparation properly for the whole trip.

During the trip I realised that I had made a big mistake, but luckily I got away with it. What I had done wrong when we had left Inverkip was that I had stayed awake all night. This was because I thought we were going to Bangor, but as I said the fog fell and I did not get to bed. This was very irresponsible of me. By the time we got to Ardglass I was falling asleep on my feet. Luckily, because there were four other very good sailors on board, we got into Ardglass with no problem. Had this just been Colette and I, it may have been a very different story. As a skipper, it is important you get as much sleep as possible. So if the banana does hit the fan, at least you are not worn out before you start. I came back from the Ireland trip knowing, in my own mind, I wanted to do the Arc. But I still never told anyone as there was still a deep fear of going to sea for that length of time. Later that year, I made my decision to ask Colette. I think deep down inside I was hoping she would say no and then I could just say I did not want to leave Colette that long. I picked my moment to ask her.

It was on a day that we had just had a fairly bad passage, from Minorca over to Majorca on 'Myrtle'. What happened was, we were on an anchorage at Cuitadella at the north end of Minorca. The weather had gone round and was getting bad. The anchorage we were in had no shelter and we had rocks right at the back of the boat. We had to make a move. So we decided to go around to the next bay and try and get some shelter. Had we stayed at the anchorage we were in, I felt we would surely have been put on the rocks. As we got out of the bay we were in, the waves were about four metres high and the big yellow ferry had stopped outside. I asked Colette if she fancied a fast crossing to Majorca, as the wind was perfect for it. We would have it right on our starboard quarter. We were well reefed and flying down the waves. It was very strange, one minute we could see the big huge yellow ferry and the next minute it would be gone behind a wave. The waves were getting higher. But although 'Myrtle' is only twenty seven foot long, she was taking it great. I was happier to stay out than to go in and look for an anchorage. Knowing the wind forecast was getting worse, Colette was happy to go for it. As she had not had that much bad weather sailing she wanted to see what it was like.

We set our course for Majorca, put another reef in the main and let a small amount of gib out. We were flying along like a train. The rain started hammering down on the boat and the black clouds were coming down to meet the water. The noise was incredible, the wind was blowing 40 knots over the deck and the waves were chasing us. Occasionally one would break right over our back. I remember at one stage, Colette was taking off her knickers and I said "There's no time for that," but she said she was so wet she could not stand them anymore.

We were absolutely soaking wet and flying down the waves. At one point I remember Colette asking God to help us. We had a fantastic trip across, doing thirty five miles in just four and a half hours. It was that night when we went for a meal in Puerto Polenca, that I asked Colette if she would like to do the Arc. I was very surprised when she said yes, and we decided to look for a bigger boat and try some longer passages. We had an agreement that if either of us were not happy, we would sell the big boat and stick to day-sailing.

We told our friends and family what we were thinking.

Our son thought it was a great challenge and was for us doing it, but most of the rest of our family were not very happy about the idea. But, as it was nearly two years away, they sort of took it with a pinch of salt. Some of our friends thought that it was all talk and would never happen. But the couple that had bought half of our boat were very encouraging. We had more or less made up our minds that we would do Arc 2000, as this would fit in with our son going to university.

The 1998 season was coming to an end and my partner in 'Myrtle' and I decided we would take the boat back to the mainland. So we planned a trip from Majorca to Barcelona for the last week in October. We had a very good passage across; just one little mishap. About 2 o'clock in the morning we were sailing along fine. One of the crew had gone down to make some supper. It was a lovely night when, all of a sudden, we were knocked flat to the water. Our friend down below had the supper all over him. At first I thought we had hit something, but then I realised it was the wind. It had come straight down the Gulf of Lyon and hit us at about 35 knots straight out of the blue. We quickly got reefed down and under control and had a good sail for the rest of the trip, just a little faster than we really wanted. We arrived in Barcelona at about 5 o'clock in the morning and it was still dark. But Barcelona is so big that you can make your way in in the dark quite easily. Just watch out for the fishing boats coming out; there are a lot of them. Barcelona is a great place to leave the boat for the winter and there is always a lot going on in the city.

During that winter, Colette and I went out looking at lots of different boats. We knew what we were looking for, ha ha, or at least we thought we did. But how wrong we were. When you are out there day-sailing and not mixing with long-haul cruising boats, there are lots of things that you never talk, or hear, about. I will go into some of these things later in more detail. But I wish I had known about them when I was buying our boat, as the boat I bought had only ever been used as a day-boat and was not geared up for long-haul cruising. Things like, water maker, solar panels, wind generator, trailing generator, SSB radio, pactor modem, breadmaker, large battery banks, battery management system, non-slip surfaces, charts, pilots etc, etc.. The list goes on. If you can buy a boat that has already done an Atlantic crossing you will save a lot of time and money over buying a boat that has only been used for short trips. We knew that we wanted a fourty to fourty five foot boat with a lot of weight and built by a reputable manufacturer. We wanted a centre cockpit boat with a good owners' cabin. We looked at lots of boats at the Boat Show. After the show, we made a decision to buy a Moody.

It was funny, whilst we were at the London Boat Show we were looking at the Hallsberg Rasseys and the salesman was looking at my clothes. I have never been a flashy dresser and he went on appearance. The fool. We were about to buy a boat from him but he did not have the time of day for us.

We found a boat advertised in one of the magazines. It was in El Campello. What a coincidence, this was the marina where we launched 'Myrtle' two years earlier. We had arranged to go out to Barcelona with our friends, to pick up 'Myrtle' and drive to Croatia. We arranged to view "'Ciao Moody'" at El Campello at the same time as we were in Barcelona. We got an inland flight down to Alicante, and we were reasonably happy with what we found, even though we knew that we would have to spend a lot of money on her to get her ready for long-haul cruising. But, basically, the boat had only one owner from new and we believed that he had looked after her reasonably well. It is a funny thing, buying a boat. You really have to take what the previous owner says as being true and hope that, as you go from marina to marina, you don't learn a different story. We had a full survey carried out on the boat from an English company that was based in Gibraltar. Although we incurred a lot more expense in the surveyors travelling costs, we were able to talk to the surveyor in english.

The survey came back and there was nothing wrong

with the boat other than one or two minor things. So we agreed to buy 'Ciao Moody', a Moody 425. Now the plan was really on to do the Arc in year 2000.

After we had been to view 'Ciao Moody', we caught the return flight back to Barcelona to pick up 'Myrtle' and take her to Croatia. We drove out of Spain, through the south of France and Monte Carlo through to Italy. While we were going through Monte Carlo we had one of the wheel bearings go on the trailer. Of all the places to go, right in the centre of Monte Carlo. We managed to find a parking space and changed the bearing. Our trailer was a six wheel trailer so it was no big deal to have one bearing go as she ran fairly well on five wheels. That was the only set back and we were soon back on our way to Croatia. We launched the boat at the north end of the Adriatic at a place called Vodice.

It is a beautiful place and the hospitality from the local people was great. The only problem there is, it is a bit like Windermere; it rains a lot during March and April. This was where I got my famous blue feet. Yes, blue feet.

I suppose I had better explain. I have been wearing the same type of deck shoes for about five years. They are very expensive, but last and can usually take all sorts of weather. The ones I normally wear are brown leather but, for some reason , I thought I would have a change and buy a blue pair. As there are not many blue cows around they have to be dyed blue. Well, the dye had not cured too well. I do not wear socks with these deck shoes and, one day the rain was running down the streets and my shoes and feet were soaked. I was not bothered about the shoes as I knew they would dry O.K. But, to my horror, when I took them off at the end of the day, my feet were bright blue. All of the dye had run onto my feet and would not wash off. I had blue feet for about 6 months. I wrote to the manufacturer of the shoes and explained. I have a good sense of humour but this was pushing it a bit too far. They apologised and sent me a new pair of shoes straight away.

We returned to the U.K. and started to make plans to go out to 'Ciao Moody'. It was like starting all over again, as we didn't take anything off 'Myrtle'. The previous owner had bought a new motor home so they had taken all the crockery, pots, pans etc with them. At first, we were a bit annoyed as we couldn't even make a cup of tea. But then really, it was a good thing as all the things we bought for the galley were all Colette's choice. But be aware that fitting out a galley from start to finish will cost you about £500. So, make sure you take account of this in your budget.

Even if your previous owner is nice enough to leave all

the galley equipment on board, they may not necessarily be what your cook wants. If your cook is not happy, you will constantly get ear-ache, so you may as well do it first as last.

We spent two or three days in the marina at El Campello, just going through the boat, making lists of things we needed to buy, safety gear etc., Things like pens, pencils, paper, sharpener, stapler, ruler, Bretton -Plotter, files, charts and pilots!!! It is surprising how quickly you will spend £100 just on bits for your chart table. Then, of course, there were the bigger items that had gone for a walk, like barometer and clock; that's another £200 before you start. By the end of the week, we had spent a lot of money on little things. But it is no good if you can't sew a button on your shirt or Sellotape a rip on a chart. The other main items that had been taken from the boat were all the tools. It is definitely no use going sailing without tools, as there is always something going wrong. Try to buy good quality tools, but do bear in mind that the salt water will attack them. Whenever you buy a second hand boat please, be prepared to have to do some work, as the previous owner may not have been as good or as fussy as you are.

We quickly found that we had a slight leak on the crank shaft oil seal and a drip on the water pump. But the biggest problem that we had was that the holding tank, to the rear toilet, was a plastic bag type that had been bodged up around the connection to the bag and was dripping down under the rear bed. It was an awful smell. I thought it was Colette at first. It was a horrible job to put right, but we did it properly, replacing all pipes and had a new, solid tank made.

We spent a few days learning about the boat. Just making small manoeuvres around the marina. It was much easier than any other boat I had been on before, as she had a bow thruster, which makes manoeuvrability much easier.

We decided we would head west down towards Gibraltar. I don't know what the attraction with Gibraltar was, but I think it was the next psychological achievement. I had wanted to sail her for some time and we planned to be there for the end of the year and to perhaps winter there for 1999.

We were still having to fly home every two weeks as David was doing A levels and having interviews for universities. He had two offers. Liverpool had said he needed 1 A and 2 B's and Manchester said he needed 2 A's and 1B. We were very confident that he would make it, but still it was a very worrying time.

The first passage we made on 'Ciao Moody' was a very unusual one. We were going to Cartagena and, as we approached the corner, the lighthouse disappeared from view. I knew we were heading into fog. Soon, it was all around us. We changed our course to head out away from land a bit, and now I could play with the radar.. I had not used a radar before, so it was a good time to learn how to use it and, I must say, they are fantastic in fog. It is very comforting to know where the other boats are, especially when you can scan out sixteen miles. We were in the fog for about four hours.

As we made our way down and were approaching Cartagena, I saw on the radar, a very fast boat coming towards us, so I altered course slightly. But so did she; and she was coming right for us. I altered again and so did she. I knew she was going to hit us. She was not that big but she was fast. As she got closer on the radar screen she slowed down, but was still on course to hit us. I went up on deck and took the wheel from Colette. All of a sudden, a large black boat appeared out of the fog with bright pink balloon fenders. Over their tannoy we heard something said in Spanish, and then in English, "Customs. Hold your course". As it came alongside I said to Colette, "Oh, they must be coming to guide us into Cartagena" But then I realised that the man on the front of the boat was pointing a machine gun at us, shouting something in Spanish. Two customs officers jumped aboard our boat as they came alongside, pointing hand guns at me. I quickly realised this was no joke. They were for real.

They kept shouting, "Contraband, contraband". I put my hands in the air, as one man came right up to me with his gun. He could speak a little English and I said, "There's no need for a gun. There is only my wife and I on board and we don't have any guns". Thankfully they put their guns away and asked what we were doing out in the fog. I told them we were going to Cartagena. They were then quite nice with us and explained they were looking for drugs and illegal immigrants. They searched the boat and checked our passports and boat papers. But, I must say, they were very courteous and polite with us, it was just a pity they approached us the way they did. I suppose they don't know what they are going to meet with these days.

We left the boat at Cartagena as I wanted to order a new water pump and crank shaft oil seals while I was at home, and Cartagena was a good place for me to do the work. We also decided to buy some new electronics; plotter, CD player, navtex weather, fax etc. I went back with one of my friends, who was a good joiner, as Colette had to stay at home whilst David was doing his exams. They were going to join us as soon as they were finished. My friend got stuck into taking the chart table apart and fitting all the new equipment we had purchased. I took the front off the engine and rebuilt it with a new water pump, crank shaft oil seal, timing belts, fan belts and replaced the timing pulley gear to a stainless steel one instead of plastic. My friend did a great job at the chart table area. You could never tell that the whole thing had been rearranged with new gear, it was such a good job.

We got all the jobs done that we had set out to do, and sailed up to meet Colette and David. He had finished all his exams, so we just had to wait for his results.

We had some good weeks' sailing around the Spanish coast, meeting lots of different people. We found that in the marinas, we were being put with other boats of our size. People would ask where we were going, what our plans were etc. When we told them we were thinking of doing Arc 2000 we had some very mixed views. Some would say that they had done the Arc in previous years and had enjoyed it. Others would ask why we wanted to go with the Arc as they thought you should go independently and save the money that the Arc charges. There were a lot of different opinions so we made a decision to go and find out for ourselves. Instead of putting the boat away for the winter, we would sail to Las Palmas in the Canary Islands and see for ourselves what Arc 1999 was all about.

David received his A level results in august of that year and got 2A's and 2 B's. So he had what he need to go to medical school at Manchester University. We were all very pleased and went out to 'Myrtle' in Croatia to celebrate. Although we still enjoyed 'Myrtle', it was very different to 'Ciao Moody' and we were definitely getting to like big boat sailing rather than day-sailing. When we got back to the U.K. David went off to university and is still enjoying every minute of it.

We were then faced with the question of whether we should sell our house or not. We never really wanted to become live aboards, but we were now spending more time on the boat than we were at home. With David now at 'Uni', we were free to spend as much time away as we liked. We decided to keep our home in the lakes, so if David wanted to come home during holidays etc., he could. But also, Colette and I feel much better knowing that if we want we can give up any time and go home.

The next thing we had to sort out was what crew we were going to have crossing the Atlantic. There are lots of horror stories about people who have taken crew they don't really know. They get five days out to sea and find they have a psycho, a manic-depressive or even worse a smoker on board!!!

We considered going on our own. But then we thought that if one of us took ill or had a fall or something, it would be a big problem. So we decided to ask our friends who shared 'Myrtle' with us, if they would like to join us. This was not really their thing, they enjoy good anchorages, shorter legs and relaxing evenings. The thought of spending twenty five nights at sea needed some consideration. Rather than commit themselves to doing the crossing, they asked if they could do the trip to the Canaries with us in September 1999, which was a crossing of six hundred miles, and would take about five to six days. They wanted to see if they enjoyed this trip first. So we made plans to leave from Cadiz to Lanzarote for the first week in October. I was reading a lot about Arc 1999 and knew the name of a lot of the boats that had entered. I had read about something called Arc Net and how Pre Arc Net was starting on Channel 6320 chz USB. This did not mean a lot to me at this stage, but the more I read about SSB radio, (single side band) the more I was interested in it. This is a radio system where you can communicate around the world with a lot of different people and coastal stations. I wanted to know more and more about it. I decided to go to Fleetwood Nautical College and do a long-range radio operators course. I eventually passed with difficulty. It is a very hard course. But I know I can honestly say that an SSB Radio is the best piece of kit on a boat and I have no hesitation in saying that.

Colette and I carried on down through Spain and on to Gibraltar. It was not all what we expected. But we had a good time there, going to see the apes, and the booze is cheap. But there is not much more than that there, except the ex-pats. In fact we got our lesson in code flag etiquette in Gib. We had arrived in the marina with our yellow Q flag as the pilot book tells you to do so. Q flag is for customs meaning nothing to declare. But I also still had our Spanish courtesy flag up, as it had been all season. As we got tidied up on the jetty in the marina, a voice came from another boat. "Excuse me, we are British, old chap, so please take down that Spanish flag!" So we were still getting it wrong. You will find when you go to Gibraltar that the Gibraltarians do not like the Spanish!!

We were not too keen on the boatyard at Gibraltar, and someone had recommended the boat yard at Puerto Sherry at Cadiz. So we thought this would be a good place to have the boat anti-fouled for the year. There was an American couple on board our boat the night before we were due to leave Gibraltar. They asked us to join them the following night but we explained we were planning to leave the following morning. The lady said, in shock, "You can't leave tomorrow. It's Friday 13th". We told her that was a lot of superstitious nonsense. We got up early the next morning to leave. Colette left the boat to go to the shower. The next thing I heard was a thump and then groaning. She had tripped over somebody's electric cable and had fell flat on her face and hurt her hand and her knees. O.K. it was Friday 13th and we ended up joining the Americans that night for a drink. We left for Cadiz the next day.

We had a lot of work done at Puerto Sherry. We had all of the old anti-foul removed and two coats of undercoat and three coats of anti-foul applied. We also had a new water line painted on. I think they call it a boot line. So I knew she was all ready to go. There was no more work to do, or so I thought. We decided that while she was still out of the water we would fit an SSB radio. One of the most important things with SSB is the ground plate. This is a brass plate that goes under the boat to ground the radio and whilst we were out of the water was an ideal time to fit it. You have to drill two holes through the bottom of the boat after you have fitted the radio.

We were waiting to be put back in the water when Colette noticed there was water coming down the back steps of the boat. We traced the leak back and found that the shower tank in the back locker, which someone had fitted in the past, was pouring water out. If the boat had been in the water we probably would not have noticed this leak. We often thought that we were using a lot of water. But when you are marina-hopping you just refill your water on a daily basis. But imagine running out of water two days into the crossing to the Canaries. We quickly fitted an in-line stop tap and have a rule now that it is only switched on when showering.

The boat went back in the water and now we were ready to go, except for the nerves. We got a forecast and stayed another day and, the next day the same thing happened. I knew we had to get out or nerves were going to get the better of us. We got a five day forecast and the weather in the north of Biscay was getting worse and was going to move south later in the week. The next day it was time to go, or I think we still would have been there. Just as we were about to leave we met a couple on the wall by the office, who asked where we were heading for. We told them Lanzarote and they told us their horror story, about how bad the sea was out there and how they turned around and came back a year ago, never to go again. This was all I needed but they said they had great admiration for us and wished us well. We were going to Lanzarote six hundred and eighty miles away, and it felt as if we were going to the end of the earth.

Well that was it, we were off. We were going across the Bay of Cadiz and out to sea. The wind was nicely coming over our shoulder and was between 15 - 29 knots. This is what I had been waiting for for so long. We had the Autohelm on and were going well.

About fifteen hours into the trip, it started getting horribly rough. I thought all the maintenance was done and that there was nothing else to do but, how wrong I was. Our problems started when the alarm on the Autohelm started going off. We switched off the Autohelm and started to steer by hand. We were well into the night and it was very, very dark. I was not sure what was going on with the Autohelm. Shortly after that, the instrument alarms were going. I knew then we had an electrical fault. I thought about turning around but we were running down a big sea and the wind was behind us. I knew that if I turned around the wind would be right on our nose. The other choice was to alter course and go to Morocco, but with two females on board I did not fancy that. I thought I would just have to hand steer until daylight and then I would find the problem. Then our lights started to go. I knew then that it was the batteries. The batteries in bank two (the domestic bank) were as flat as flukes. This was the first time they had gone as long without being charged up. This is one of the problems with day-boats; as the batteries are being charged up every night in marinas you don't get to know that the batteries are shot! I thought that all we had to do was switch from battery bank one to two and start the engine to recharge the batteries.

Unfortunately, battery one had flattened as well. The wind and sea were increasing and we now had no electrics. We had a fridge full of food and the fridge was now off. I needed to slow the boat down. We were going very fast down the waves and had no lights on. I reefed down again. But, at one stage, we were still doing 11 knots. The sea was about thirty feet high behind us and the wind was blowing about 30 - 35 knots. We were all getting very tired, as we were getting into the second night. I knew I had to get some power and get the engine running. I clipped myself on and made my way to the back of the boat to get the petrol generator from the aft locker. It was only a small 700 watt generator but I knew it would give us lights and put something into the batteries. As I was tying down the generator, I was looking up at a wall of water behind us. I kept thinking it was going to break over us, but 'Ciao Moody' just kept surfing down the waves. With hardly any sails up, just a tiny bit of gib and a small amount of main, I finally got the genny running and this gave us lights and Autohelm. It also meant we could get some sleep in small amounts; I knew I still had to get the engine running . In the end, I decided that if I took the battery from the bow thruster, which was under the bed in the bow of the boat, to the back of the boat I could jump start the engine. This is not an exercise I would like to do again in a hurry. I finally got it unbolted; I can tell you, being up in the bow of the boat in a big, following sea, is not the nicest of places to be. Then, having to walk from one end to the other of a bucking boat with a battery in your hands is hard work. But the plan worked. I got the engine running and this was putting new life into the batteries.

Despite all the trouble with the batteries we were flying along at about 9 knots. We were actually making two hundred miles per day, and were looking good to make Lanzarote in three and a half days. I left the engine running now, which was also helping with our speed. The only question now was did we have enough diesel? The next problem arose when I next went to do our four hourly engine check. I found that the new seal that I had put in the water pump had gone again and we were pumping water into the boat. The bilge was filling up fast. I thought it best not to alarm the others. So I just told Colette we had a water problem and it was important to pump out the bilges every thirty minutes. It is important that you tell one other person that you have a problem in case something happens to you. Because of our situation I altered our course to Sociedad on the Island of Graciosa. This was just at the tip of Lanzarote, about fourty miles closer than Calero, our intended destination. We were hoping to make it before night fall but just missed it and got in about 10 o'clock at night. It is a very bad entrance but we managed it O.K. We carried on down to Lanzarote the next day.

We were all very tired and had had a worrying trip. But I felt as though I could have carried on sailing forever. I remember, as I was going to sleep that night, Colette thanked me for getting us there safely. She said she felt like carrying on across the Atlantic. It was good to hear her say it. Each day we had been talking to people from Arc boats on the SSB. But it was not very good because of the batteries flattening. One of the boats we had been talking with was in Graciosa and they lent us some diesel in case we needed it. This is the spirit of the Arc, everyone goes out of their way to help you.

Our friends went home from Lanzarote and Colette and I carried on to Las Palmas, after we had repaired the water pump and charged up all the batteries. When we arrived at Las Palmas we had all our electrics checked and found that there was a link between battery banks 1 and 2. This is why bank one had also gone flat. We had a new set of batteries fitted and also a Sterling management system fitted. This allows you to see exactly what is going in and out of your battery and how much power each bank has in them. The new domestic battery bank had 375 AH and we hade 125 AH in battery bank one for starting our engine.

We also now have a wind generator that gives us, on average, about 15A per hour. We also have four solar panels with 55w in each, and in total they give us 10A per hour in sunlight. We also have a trailing generator which gives about one amp per knot, so at 6 knots per hour, you get about 6 amps per hour. But you do lose a little bit of boat speed, about .5 knots per hour. This does not sound a lot but on an Atlantic crossing you lose about two days. That's not all you lose; I'll tell you that one later on in the book.

We had a fabulous time in Las Palmas in 1999 and it was very upsetting to see all the boats sail off to the Caribbean and for us to just go back into the marina. It was such a good atmosphere and we met a lot of wonderful people. At one stage we felt like going with them. But we had made our plans for year 2000 and not 1999. The people who advise you not to go with the Arc have their own reasons, but I would say to you, if you are not sure, go to Las Palmas in November and make up your own mind. We were 100% sure that we were going on Arc 2000 and paid our fees to World Cruising as soon as Arc 1999 had left.

We spent the winter cruising the Canaries. We went to Tenerife , Gomera, Lanzarote and Fuerta Ventura. We came home to be with David and the rest of the family at Christmas and left the boat at Tenerife. It was when we were at home that our friends told us that they did not enjoy long-haul sailing and would not be joining us for Arc 2000. We were glad that they told us then, as this gave us time to look for someone else.

We did not want another lady in the galley as Colette had made her mind up she wanted to do all the cooking for the crossing. So, we asked two male friends. They said they would like to come to the Canaries to do a trial trip and make their decision afterwards. We arranged for this trip to be in early April. Before that came one of my best cock-ups yet. We were in Los Gigantes at the bottom of Tenerife, in January, waiting for some friends from the Boat Club who were coming to join us for a week. I had been doing my maintenance. I had taken out the water filter to clean it and forgot to switch the water back on. So our guests arrived and we headed out of Gigantes to Gomera.

We were in very little wind, with the engine running. We were very lucky that Colette was filling in her half hourly log sheet and noticed that the water temperature dial was showing 105 degrees when it normally shows 83. I quickly switched off the engine and when I went down below the back cabin had filled with smoke. I had completely wrecked the water pump, but fortunately had not done any other damage to the engine. This is another good reason to use your log sheets. We tied our dinghy to the side of 'Ciao Moody' and made our way back to the marina at Gigantes with the outboard on the dinghy. What a good start with our two friends from the boat club. But as I have said many times before, the man that made no mistakes has not been to sea before. We fitted the spare water pump and got going again the next day. The rest of the week went very well and we had a good time.

We had to go back to the U.K. as we had booked a Ships Captain's medical course in Southampton. We both passed. We felt that this was a very good course to take as, if one of us or our crew took ill we would at least have some idea of what to do. It was a great course, it showed us how to give injections and to stitch up cuts and to deal with a lot of injuries that could happen on a boat. Burns, falls, head injuries etc. I would recommend anyone to go and get some basic information and first aid training. As out there, you really are on your own.

We carried on sailing in the Canaries until our two male friends came out to do their trial week. The weather was forecast to be a bit heavy but both men had been sailing for a long time and were very good sailors. So bad weather did not bother them too much. We spent the first day getting to know the boat and then decided to go over to Lanzarote before leaving for Madeira, about three hundred miles north. We had been out for about three hours when one of the men went down below to get a drink. The wind was blowing about 25-30 knots and the sea state was about ten to fifteen feet and lumpy. My friend moved the salad bowl with one hand and grabbed a drink with the other hand. At that split second the boat took a knock by a wave and he flew across the boat, landing on the corner of the chart table on his ribs. He immediately fell to the floor, making a lot of noise. Sods law is that if I hadn't been on the medical course it probably wouldn't have happened. Fortunately, I knew what to do, as we had done broken ribs on the course two weeks earlier. We had to alter our course now and got to Mogan on Gran Canaria to get my friend to a doctor. He had broken three of his ribs and was very sore. We changed the itinerary for this trip and just took it easy. We went to Calero in Lanzarote and spent a few days there, and Fuerta Ventura, and went back to Tenerife at the end of the fortnight. Our friends went home to make the decision whether to do the Atlantic crossing with us or not. The friend who had taken the fall made the decision not to join us and our other friend said yes. So now we were wondering whether to go with just the three of us.

It was now May and time was running out for finding crew. We were at home and our son had come home for the weekend. We were telling him about our crew situation. He said he knew a lad in Ambleside who had just been made redundant and was looking to take some time out. He had never been on a boat in his life! We arranged to meet the lad out at Fuerta Ventura with our David, a few week later. We said he could come out for a week's holiday to see if he liked sailing or not. At the end of the week he had made his decision to come back out two weeks later and do some more sailing.

He was a very fast learner and a great help on the boat. He would get up and work all day, every day, and never complain. I did not even have to ask him to do things, he just got on and cleaned and maintained things every day. One of the things he was very good at was sleeping! The job he had just left was night shift work, so he could stay up at night and sleep all day if needed. But we needed to give him some longer passages to see what he would be like, so for his first trip we went to Madeira and then Porto Santo. I wanted to see what he would be like over a few nights, so we decided to go back to the Med for a few weeks, and start all over again and meet the Arc 2000 boats coming down.

It is a very hard passage back to the Med. The wind is mainly northerly and the swell is also from the north. At one stage we had 40 knots from the north and had to sail a long way west to keep the boat moving. But our new crew member was loving every moment of it. We eventually made our landfall five days later at Lagos in Portugal. I knew then that he was the right man for the trip. He fitted in very well on our boat. Everybody that we met liked him. He really was a very likeable lad with a very pleasant personality.

I remember Bob's first night shift. I wanted to leave him up top on his own but, rather than just leave him, I stayed up with him until about midnight. We sat and talked about what to do if he was to see a ship in the night. But there are not that many ships out there, believe it or not. I went down to bed and told Bob to call me if he saw anything. About two hours later, Bob called me to say he could see a ship. I got dressed and came up. The ship he could see was a dot on the horizon. I did not want to bring him down for calling me, even though the ship was about fifteen miles away. He had done exactly what I had asked him and called me as soon as he saw something. We decided we would use this ship as an exercise. So, I told Bob to take a bearing on it and to go down and fix the radar cursor on it. At this stage, all we could see was a white light, so I told Bob to use the binoculars to see if he could see its lights to make out which way it was heading. One of the rules of our boat is that if you see something, you must take a bearing on it every fifteen minutes and also continue to do a 360 degree lookout with the binoculars. It is Sod's law that while you are busy looking at one ship, another one sneaks up behind your back. The next time we took a bearing on the ship it was exactly the same and though we could see a lot of white lights through the binoculars, we still could not see any coloured lights.

But we could see on the radar that it was a very big ship and it was now only 5 miles away. So, now it was time to try and make contact with this ship on the radio. We tried our normal call, "Big ship, big ship in position .... this is small sailing boat on your bow" We tried this three or four times, but unfortunately nobody came back. We could now see the port-hand light amongst the many large white lights. The bearing was still exactly the same, and we were on a perfect collision course. I really couldn't believe it. I have been out there at night many times now and hardly ever see another ship; this was Bob's first night shift. Had we held our course we would certainly have been run down. We now tacked to starboard to go down her port side. We continued to call her on the radio but I don't think there was anybody on watch. We could see as we went down the side of the ship, that the crew were all busy working on deck. It had lights like a football pitch.

Once we had cleared her, we tacked back to our original course. A few minutes later we could hear another ship calling her but, again there was no reply. This gave us great confidence in our new crew member. Not only does he stay awake but he does exactly as you tell him.

Since leaving Lanzarote, we had been trying to catch fish. I felt that, on the crossing, it would be a great advantage if we could catch fresh fish. We had trawled a line for about two hundred and fifty miles and then, all of a sudden, the line started running off the reel. We were all up. Bob went to the back of the boat and started reeling in, only to find that we had caught a pink rubber glove. We reckoned that in all that water there must be millions of fish but only one rubber glove and we had to catch it. Well you can imagine how much stick Bob got. Two days later about 5 o'clock in the morning, I was down in bed, as I had done the 12 till 4 shift and the next thing I knew Bob was waking me up, "Excuse me, can you help me get this fish in please?" I opened one eye and said, "If it's a rubber glove, I'll kill you" Luckily for him, it was our first catch. A really nice tuna, about half a metre long. This put us all in a good mood for days, but I have to tell you, its a messy job trying to clean fish on the back of the boat.

We have now geared ourselves up with a large four inch deep plastic tray, which we have on a long lanyard. You can head, tail and clean out the fish in the tray and then easily throw all the mess over the side. Then you just wash the tray by dragging it behind the boat for a few minutes, and bring it back in on the lanyard.

We had a play around in Portugal for a few weeks and then went back into the Mediterranean, as David was coming out to Puerto Banus with his girlfriend and some of his mates, to play golf. We had a good time with David and his friends for a week or so and then we had to start to make our way back to Lagos in Portugal. Rob stayed with our son playing golf and then had a few weeks at home before coming back to do the crossing. I thought it would be good for him to go home for a few weeks, so he could be sure that he really wanted to do the Arc 2000. It turned out that he was very keen and could not wait to get back. We thought we might have a problem. While he was at home he had fallen in love, and we thought he may not come back. But he is the kind of lad that if he makes a commitment he sticks to it.

On our way back to Portugal we stopped at Puerto Sherry, Cadiz. Because we had such a good service in Puerto Sherry in 1999 we decided to go back there and have the boat lifted out and re-anti-fouled. While she was out of the water, we had a new water intake tap fitted for the water maker. The intake we were using for the water maker was too far away from the unit. We were using the same supply as the seawater tap on the sink. We found that when we put the new supply right next to the unit, it worked much better, as it was not having to pull the water so far. I will tell you more about the water maker later.

An interesting thing happened to me in Puerto Sherry, that you should perhaps take note of, and, maybe, notify your bank. I went to pay my bill for the work that had been done on my boat, only to find my credit card had been rejected. This was the first time this had ever happened to me and I could not understand why, as we have all our credit cards set up on direct debit to be settled every month. It was very embarrassing; I finally got through to somebody at the credit card centre, after listening to about ten verses of Beethoven and a recording telling me they were sorry to keep me waiting and thanking me for my patience. Patience! I was ready to kill. I was on my mobile phone at about £1 per minute.

Eventually, I got through to somebody who told me my card had been stopped as a security measure, because of our unusual movements over the past few weeks. When I explained that we were a cruising yacht in transit, they lifted the bar from my card. Apparently, it is best to inform your credit card company if you are moving about a bit to stop this from happening. I was very angry when I got to speak to the manager.

I know that security measures are to protect our best interest, but there is no need to play ten verses of Beethoven to us. But they did reimburse us £50 for phone calls, and I should think so, making me listen to that. If you don't want the same thing happening to you, just drop your credit card company a short note, letting them know your whereabouts.

We moved on to Portugal and stopped in an anchorage at Faro. Sadly, this was where we received a phone call from one of my family to say that one of my aunts had died. I wanted to go home to be with my father, as he was 85 and I knew he was very upset. Colette rang around to try and get flights. But, it was not possible to get what we needed. We also had to try to find a safe place to leave the boat. The weather was against us to go to Villamoira, the nearest marina where we could leave her. I spoke with my family, and they said there was nothing we could do and that we should not come home. This is one of the things that plays on your mind a lot when you start to do longer trips. I have spoken to lots of people about this and it seems that we all have parents and family who are getting on a bit.

We moved onto Lagos and got ready to go back to the Canaries. We met up with other Arc boats who were also on their way to Las Palmas. We were now talking on the SSB every day with boats that were coming down the Bay of Biscay to Cascai and Lagos. Bob was flying in that weekend and we were ready to go back. Well, the boat was. But I could not stop thinking about my father. I knew that he was not too good at home and I also knew he was worrying about us on top of everything else. Bob arrived, and we were about to go, doing our last minute checks, when I discovered that one of our shrouds was a bit loose. There was a good rigger on Villamoira, so we decided to go back there and have the rigging reset. It was only about thirty miles. Secretly, I was stalling. I could not tell Colette and Bob how I was feeling, but I did not want to go. In my head I was thinking of how I could tell Colette. I knew how long she had wanted to do this for and now she had become the best crew member any boat could ask for. She had cooked in all sorts of weather, kept up the welfare of the boat at all times of day and night and can do anything on the boat on her own. Young Bob had fallen in love and had still come back out to sail away for the next two months. My fourth crew member had booked his flights so as to meet us in Las Palmas in about three weeks time. I had half decided that I was going to tell Colette and Bob that night, that I was calling the whole thing off. The rigger had finished the work on the boat. So, that was it no more excuses. We said that we would leave at midday the next day. Colette and I were walking up to the shop at the top of the road when a voice from behind shouted, "David" I turned to find a friend of mine and his wife from the U.K. who were at a National Tyre Conference at one of the hotels. We arranged for them to come down to the boat later for a drink. This friend had once turned a boat over and lost it in the South China Sea in a violent tropical storm. He had also spent a lot of time sailing with Pete Goss in the services. We had a lot to talk about and he put me back in the mood.

We set sail the next day, as planned, and started our course for Madeira. We had been sailing for about ten hours and were about 80 miles out when the weather starting to blow a bit, about 25 knots from the north, and the sea started to get a little bit lumpy. Colette had finished our evening meal, cleaned up and finished for the day. Bob had gone down to bed. I was doing the 8 till12 watch, and I had not long finished getting dressed for the shift. You have to get well dressed as it is bitterly cold in the middle of the night in the Atlantic, that far north. A wave came over the boat. It was not that big really, we had had a lot bigger, but it was the final straw. I said to Colette that I was sorry, but I wanted to go back. I think at first she thought I was joking. But she knew I was upset and did not want to go on. I just wanted to go home.

Colette reminded me of our arrangement, that if one of us did not want to go on, then we would give up. But I never thought that it would be me. I turned the boat around and started to sail against the wind and sea, back to Lagos. The boat was banging down as the waves were quite high and the wind was a good 30 knots. Young Bob came up to see what was wrong and asked why we had turned around. I told him that I had had enough and was going home. He was also very shocked. I told him I would get him on a nother boat as he was now good crew. Alternatively, I would fly him out to the Caribbean for a holiday, either way, he would get to see the Caribbean, one way or another. We had a rough passage back to Lagos and got back early the next morning. I rang our son first and told him I had given up. He was not impressed but said "If that's what you want then that's O.K." The next person I rang was my father. I told him that I was coming home. I knew right away he was relieved and he said, "Oh good. I was not happy about you sailing across the Atlantic, but I was not going to stand in your way" Next I tried to ring Eric, our other crew member who was coming out to meet us at Las Palmas. He was not there because he had gone away to put his own boat away for the winter. In Lagos there is a very friendly yacht brokerage run by an English family. I asked the father to come down to the boat and put her up for sale. He was very impressed with what he saw. But I knew that with the amount of new equipment on board we were going to lose a lot of money. I had spent about £30,000 on the boat since we bought it. We got a flight the next day and went home. The first thing I did was to go and see my father. I think that one of the main things in my head was that I was scared of my dad dying whilst I was on the crossing I wouldn't even be able to attend the funeral. With missing my aunts' funeral, this was playing on my mind. My father said a few things that made me feel much better, and I think just seeing him put my mind at rest, and that he was OK. I knew that we were going to be the laughing stock of the boat club and I was finding it hard to tell anybody. I went round to speak to one of my friends, who was a lot older than me and told him how I was feeling. We had a good chat and he said a lot of things that made a lot of sense. I also rang another friend of mine; the one that had fallen and hurt his ribs. He was also a bit older than me, had been around a bit longer and been through similar things in his lifetime. He told me to get out to the boat and get going as this was a chance of a lifetime, and that it would probably never happen if I gave up now.

Colette was not very happy back at home. It was cold and wet and we had nothing to do as the last two years had been spent getting ready to sail across the Atlantic.

We had only been home for three days when the first offer was made on the boat. As I said it is in immaculate condition. It's funny really, most people think that it is a new boat and are very surprised when I tell them that it is ten years old.

Two days later, I got the second offer on the boat. Had I accepted one of the offers, I think that would have been it for ever, and this would have been the last page of this daft book that is driving me mad as I to write it. Well, there would probably never have been a book. I asked Colette if we should take the offer on the boat and she said this was the last chance, I'd got to make up my mind. I picked up the phone and bought three tickets back to Lagos, I then rang Bob and told him we were leaving on

Saturday, and asked if he was still on board. Thankfully, he said yes. I was so pleased after I had messed him around so much. As soon as we got to Lagos we went straight to the supermarket and stocked up with food and were ready to go the next morning. As we were now a week behind schedule we plotted a course straight to Las Palmas. This was seven hundred and thirteen miles. We had a fabulous sail and it only took us one hundred hours and fifteen minutes from marina to marina. The boat was performing like never before; it was as if she was talking to me.

Once we got to Las Palmas, we met up with a lot of other boats we had been talking to for a long time on the radio and it was great to put faces to the names. There were only three weeks to go now to the big day.

The first thing we did was to get booked into the local gymnasium and try to get ourselves fit. We knew where the gym was from the previous year and, when we went in to see the owners, they made us very welcome. We were like their long lost friends. The people from Las Palmas are very friendly and make the Arc boats very welcome. It is a big event to them and they go out of their way to make sure that it continues to leave from Las Palmas, year after year.

We didn't have to work on the boat as I had been maintaining her for the last two years. She was ready to go. So, we now had two weeks left before leaving and our other crew member was not coming out for another week. We were just cleaning and doing final checks. There are a lot of different seminars you can attend at Las Palmas, all arranged by the Arc. They are all very good. We had booked all of ours for the second week, once Eric had arrived, so he could also attend. While waiting for Eric to arrive, one of the jobs that we decided to do was to unpickle the water maker. I told you I would come back to the water maker. They are a fantastic piece of kit, but they are definitely female. If you don't treat them properly you will have nothing but trouble. You must run them every day to stop them from blocking up. If you can not run them every day then you must pickle them. This is done by filling and flushing the system with a biocide. You must also keep the filter clean at all times and you must never run them in a marina, as you will put diesel and other muck into the membrane. Then, you will have big trouble. But, if you look after them properly, they are fantastic. The one that we have produces 8 litres of water an hour and only uses 5 amps per hour. I have fitted ours so that I can have the water going to the main tanks or I can divert it to a plastic container. I think having this last option is the best, as I feel better being able to test the water rather than it going straight in to my tanks. I would hate it to go faulty and maybe put salt water in to the tanks.

Water was one of my main concerns. You can go for three weeks without food, but only three days without water. On our boat, there are two fourty five gallon water tanks, one on each side of the boat. They both meet in the middle, so that you only fill up from one side. They also used to empty down at the same time, but I have now put in-line taps in the pipe, so I can control how much water I take out of each tank. This way if I was to get a leak, I would only lose one tank. Although we had ninety gallons in the tank when we were leaving for the crossing, I also had one and a half litre bottles of drinking water on board, one hundred and fifty of them! We also made twenty four litres of water every day, which we put into either empty bottles or the tank for the shower. For the first ten days of the crossing I was very strict with our water. I would only allow the solar shower, which we hung up at the back of the boat. This way, I knew exactly how much water was being used. We would wash our dishes with salt water and just rinse with fresh water.

We also had four hundred cans of soft drinks on board, which meant we could each have four, every day for twenty five days. We had one hundred cans of beer; I would allow one can per person per day.

We only used ten beers on the whole crossing, and as we were refilling our bottles every day from the water maker, when we arrived at St. Lucia, after twenty one days, we had the same amount of water as when we left Las Palmas.

Electricity was my next main concern, especially after the trip we had had the year before with flat batteries. I did not want to use my engine on the crossing, I will tell you why later. So I fitted a few different forms of charging. We had 4 x 55w flexible solar panels, that in reality give out 10A per hour in total, during sunlight hours. You could say we were getting about 100A per day from the panels. We also had a wind generator that can give up to 35A per hour, according to the sales bumph, but because we were mainly running downwind, the wind generator was only giving about 3A per hour in total. We were generating about 75 amps per day. We also had a trailing generator, that does do what the sales bumph says it does. It literally gave us IA per knot per hour. So yes, you can get on average 5A per hour. So you will get 120A per day. But what the sales literature does not tell you is that the sharks like them. They don't just bite them, they rip them off the back of your boat!!

You may have read about ours. We noticed that ours had stopped charging and we pulled the propeller in to see what was wrong, only to find that the blades had been bitten off. We were carrying spare blades, so were able to get ours going again. On average we were getting about 100A per day. On top of all this we ran our 700 watt petrol generator every day for three hours. Three hours equated to one litre of petrol and during that three hours we would make water. At this time we would also make a loaf of bread in the bread maker via our 240v invertor. Also we would run our 40 amp hour battery charger. We ran all our appliances freely and, at all times, our batteries were reading full.

The reason I did not want to use my engine on the passage is that we only carry three hundred litres of diesel, although we did have another one hundred litres in containers. Even with four hundred litres this would have given us eight hundred miles at best and as we had three thousand three hundred to go, I was saving my diesel in case we had any problems towards the end of the journey or in case of an emergency where I may have needed to motor to another vessel in distress. The other reason was that there is a lot of debris floating about out there and the last thing I wanted was a fishing net or something around my propeller. We did run our engine for about one hour per day on average, to give us hot water for cleaning etc. We arrived at St. Lucia with three hundred litres of diesel still in the tanks.

We had provisions for five weeks, so we had a lot of food on board. We had lots of net bags hanging in the saloon with all our fresh vegetables in. Most fresh food lasted for about ten days, except the tomatoes, oranges and onions, which lasted until they were all eaten or until we arrived at St. Lucia. We had all our fresh meat portioned and vacuum packed in Las Palmas, and this lasted for about 15 days. As we were catching fish every day, it got to a stage were Colette was saying , "No more". All you have to do is put your line out over the back of the boat at about fifty metres with a 4" brightly coloured lure on and you will catch fish all day long. If you use a lure any bigger then be prepared to catch very big fish. We found that a 4" lure would give us, on average, fish about one metre long. We carried lots of rice, pasta and tinned meats and fruits. We had lots of food over when we arrived at St. Lucia, but this is not a bad thing, as food in the Caribbean is not cheap, so if you have the room, take as much as you can.

With one week to go, our other crew member, Eric, joined us and now we had a week of partying to do as well as attending lectures and seminars during the day. There was a different function every night of the week to attend. This, for me, was one of the biggest advantages of the Arc. The camaraderie of 2000 like minded people, all doing the same thing. The Arc is a great leveller. No matter how much money you have or don't have, or how different you all are, you all depend on each other when you are out there. The marina was absolutely bustling with atmosphere, and we went on to meet more and more people from all walks of life, and lots of different countries all doing the same thing. I think the party week before you leave is a great way of getting to know your crew, and the crew of the other boats.

The Saturday before we left was the skippers' briefing, and we went over the weather and radio net times and frequencies. I was given the job as one of the net controllers for our group. After the briefing, we went out for a really nice meal. Everybody seemed to be doing the same thing. It was like the last supper. It was a very quiet night and everybody was in bed early.

On the Sunday morning you could hear a pin drop. I think everybody had the same last minute nerves. We quickly let down our regatta code flags and filled the water tanks. At about 11 o'clock there were boats beginning to make their way out of the marina. There were thousands of people lining the harbour wall and the noise of the whistles and horns are unforgettable. I decided that we would hang back to the last. As the year before, I saw a few boats get damaged on the start line and, with twenty plus days ahead of us I could see no point in a racing start at 11.45. I told my crew that we were leaving the jetty at midday for the 1.00 start line. I told them to make their phone calls home because the phone would not work once we were out of the bay.

Eric rang his mother first, and as she was 93, it was a very hard call to make. He simply came off the phone and got on with doing something at the front of the boat. Young Bob made a call to his girlfriend and mother and was ready to go. Colette rang her mum and dad . I found it very hard to speak to them. I remember hearing Colette tell her mother and father to look after themselves and that she would never forgive herself if anything happened to them while she was away. Then she said, "We never tell each other how much we care" She then proceeded to tell her parents how much she loved them, promising that she would look after herself. The tears were running down her cheeks. I knew it was time to go. I had not rang my father. In fact my father did not know I was in Las Palmas. He still thought the boat was for sale in Lagos. I was not going to tell him any different. I did not want to upset him, I had never deceived him before. When Colette came off the phone I went to ring him but I could not do it. I rang our David and told him to look after himself and to ring his grandad (my dad) once a week. He asked me whether he was to try to get a message to me if anything happened to my dad whilst I was away. I told him there would be no point as we would not be able to turn back after the first few days out. I came off the phone and told the lads. "If you don't get the ropes off now, they won't be coming off"

We motored out of the marina in a line of boats with thousands of well wishers on the harbour wall, waving and blowing horns. We had "You'll Never Walk Alone" playing from our CD through the outside speakers on the boat. As we made our way out to the line, we had about twenty minutes to wait for the start of Arc 2000. We set our sails and sailed away from the rest of the fleet so as not to get involved with the line. It was a fantastic site to see two hundred and twenty five boats all waiting to go to the same place. At 12.50, I turned the boat around and told the lads to set the sails. The gun went off and we crossed the line a few minutes later. I called the race officer on VHF and thanked them for a wonderful start. I had one more thing to do. I picked the phone up and rang my dad. I simply said, "We're off dad" He said, "Where to?" I said, "The Caribbean, we have just crossed the start line. I will ring you in three weeks" I couldn't say anything else as I had a big lump in my throat, so I quickly handed the telephone to Colette and she quickly explained.

People had told me that the crossing could be boring. I think that is down to the skipper. I was very conscious of making sure that our trip would not be a boring one. We had a set of jobs that had to be done every day and we planned different things to look forward to.

The first thing that was planned was our 'Out One Week Party'. Then we had plans for a half-way party, then a two week out party. A thousand to go, and then of course, the big arrival. We got off to a great start. We crossed the line and made our way down towards the end of the island of Gran Canaria. We had been on the go about one hour and I decided to come off the helm and gave the wheel to Eric to do the 2 till 6 watch. The first thing Eric said when he took the wheel was that the steering felt heavy. I felt the wheel again and said it was as normal. But Eric had been on another Moody two weeks before and said that the steering on that had been much lighter.

We were among about one hundred and fifty boats and, as we went into the night we could see lights for miles around us. As we got into the next day, we could only see about twenty boats and on the second night about ten and the third day only about three. The Arc Radio Net was great. Every day at 3 o'clock UT time our group radioed in their position. It was very reassuring to know that there were boats all around you even though you could not see them.

Our first week flew by very fast and soon we were

looking forward to our half-way party. The wind was mainly behind us and we were running goose-winged down wind. We flew the spinnaker by day and a small main and full gib by night. This gave us a good comfortable rig and about 5.5 knots. The boat constantly rolled from side to side every single day of the journey. This is why you need lots of non-slip mats. We found that eating out of large plastic bowls was much easier than trying to eat from plates. Every day, we noticed, that the boats that were using twin head sails, poled out, were pulling away from us by about fifteen to twenty miles per day. They were also able to leave that rig set up day and night. We tried flying our storm jib off the emergency forestay but, as we only had one pole this was not as good. We will definitely use two poles and twin head sails next time.

We spent about one hour a day sorting out the rubbish. We put all food waste over the side. We washed all plastic bags and boxes and cut them flat and packed them into plastic bags. You will be surprised how much you can get into a large bag after you have cleaned and flattened everything. We tied the bags down on the front of the boat. This way, any smell would be blown away as we were down wind. Make sure you have plenty of large plastic bags. Also make sure you have plenty of anti-bacterial soap in the heads. Don't be embarrassed to ask your crew to make sure they wash their hands frequently, and always after using the toilet. Make sure your crew are washing everyday, as the last thing you want is an upset stomach on board. One of the jobs I did every day myself, was to wash the cockpit with a disinfectant spray.

Before we knew it, we were having our half-way party. This was a beautiful five course meal Colette had made for us, complete with a bottle of champagne. It's funny how easily accidents can happen. As I opened the bottle of champagne I took off the wire. The cork shot straight out of the bottle and skimmed Bob's head. One inch lower and it would have taken his eye out. You can imagine how much of a problem that would have been halfway across the Atlantic. We were very lucky.

Back home, our friends and family were monitoring us on the Internet, every inch of the way. Every day the boat positions were reported back to Cowes and then World Cruising would display them on the Internet. One of our boat club friends was getting our position every day and informing our families of our progress.

We had very little go wrong on our trip. We had a spinnaker sheet snap. It just cut against the pole end. This was with constant rubbing in the same place. A pole with a pulley in the end would have been better. Another day, we managed to get the spinnaker under the boat, but thankfully, the weather was calm and we were able to get it back without a problem.

We had quite a scary moment one night at about 3 o'clock. I was in bed when, all of a sudden, there was a lot of banging going on up on deck. Eric was calling me to come up. I jumped up, quickly dressed and put on my harness, as no one is allowed out of the saloon at night without being clipped on. When I got up I found that the second headsail we had put up on the emergency forestay had come off the snap shackle, which had come undone. This was a big problem, as the sail was hanked on to the wire and as it had come away from the deck, the whole sail was flying in front of the boat. Every time it came down, the pulley shackle would bang against the deck. I thought about turning the boat around into the wind, but we were in a big forwarding sea and the wind was about 25 knots. The wire and shackle came down, so I grabbed hold of it. But it was hurting my hands, so I had to let go. I put on my big Goretex gloves and the next time it came down I grabbed it. The problem was every time I grabbed it, it would start to set and then it was pulling me over the side. Although I was clipped on and had hold of the shrouds, I still could not hold it. There was far too much power. I asked Eric to get Bobby up.

Now this alone is not an easy job, as Bob sleeps for

England and without a doubt, he is best at sleeping. Eric woke Bob up, but now I had to wait until he put on his harness and lifejacket. While I was waiting the wire was whipping around all over the place. It came down again and I managed to get a rope on to the pulley and then by releasing the sheet, I was able to get it back on to the boat. Bob and I were able to put it away, then we were ready for a nice cup of tea!!!

I would make a cup of tea on most shift changeovers, as I think the person coming on wakes up properly with a cup of tea in his hand. Even when the shift was changing from Eric to Bob I would still get up and check the changeover.

One night, Bob and Eric committed a major offence on the boat, which led to a crown court hearing the next day. One of them had eaten the last chocolate biscuit. Colette had asked, when she went to bed, if we would save her one. Eric had accused Bob of eating it. So Bob became the accused. I was the judge and Colette and Eric were the jury. Bob said that it was not a fair trial, as one of the jurors was a party to the offence and the other member of the jury was the person who had suffered the loss. I agreed with the accused and dismissed Eric and Colette from the jury, and appointed Colette and Eric instead. I told Bob that if he pleaded guilty we would reduce his sentence to keel hauling in Rodney Bay,

St. Lucia. The original sentence we were thinking of was no showers for a week. I think with the way the hearing was going, even with the new jury, he knew he was on a loser. So he pleaded guilty and agreed to a keel hauling. When he was asked if he had anything to say, he said, "Yes, it was bloody Eric that ate the biscuit" it was a great trial. We had good fun and laughed for about an hour and a half. But Bob never was going to win, as it was me that ate the last biscuit. Sorry boys.

On other days, we would have video karaoke and we had to sing along with a karaoke CD that we had brought along with us. The video camera was always stuck in your face. This was also great fun.

I had a night when I was on watch, when I was willabied!! Well I think that is what the American lady called it. I was just sitting there, writing a part of this book, when I looked behind me to see a big black cloud. It seemed to be running after us. I quickly reefed down the main even further than it was already reefed, and rolled in the genoa even more. The next thing I knew, it was raining with drops the size of golf balls. I was absolutely soaked to the skin and standing in about three inches of water. Then, within thirty minutes, there was a very warm wind that dried everything up in minutes. Small tropical squalls are amazing things. Later when I was speaking on the SSB radio and telling someone what had happened, this American lady came on to the channel and told me I had been willabied. Apparantly, they call these types of squalls a willaby.

We had another scary moment one night, at about 2 o'clock in the morning, it was very dark and I was fast asleep downstairs. Eric came down quietly and started to shake me. He whispered, "Can you come please". I put my life jacket and harness on and went up. It was very quiet and flat calm. I said, "What's going on Eric?"

He said, "I think I can hear something."

I listened with him for a few minutes but could hear nothing. All of a sudden a large spray of water went into the air along side us. It stunk of fish or cod liver oil. We were surrounded by whales. They started blowing all around us. It's a funny feeling when everything is going so well, knowing that at any minute now, you might have a big hole in the boat and be on the way to the bottom if one of these whales starts to lose its temper. I quickly and quietly asked Bob and Colette to get up and put on their harnesses and life jackets without making a noise. We put on our engine and started to motor away 90 degrees to my original course and, thankfully, the whales carried on their course. They really do rule the sea.

Before long we only had a thousand miles left to go and every day on the radio, we were starting to hear of boats that had arrived in St. Lucia. I had planned to arrive on Monday morning and I was not going to rush or do anything different to get there earlier. I was being asked to put the engine on to try to get there for Sunday or to fly the kite longer, till dusk, to make more speed. But I told them my ETA was Monday at midday and that was not going to change. It had taken me a long time to get ready for this trip and I was enjoying it. I felt like I could go on forever and I wanted to keep going. I did not want to stop. In fact at one stage, when I was asked to put the engine on, I answered, "The next time I am asked to rush this trip, I will set a course for Argentina", which, at this point, was another 2,500 miles away. We only had 600 miles to go to St. Lucia. I think all on board got the message, as I was not asked again. The final run in was with about three other boats that were close to us. The last two days, we were only one mile to the side of a catamaran. It was quite nice to be able to see and talk to another boat.

On the Sunday morning with only one hundred and twenty miles to go, I knew that our ETA was going to be correct. As I still had nearly a full tank of diesel, we were nicely sailing along. Colette was on watch, and Eric and Bob were down below, sleeping. Colette's eyes are not the best in the world, so she tends to use the binoculars a lot when she is on watch.

Suddenly, Colette asked me "What's that in the water?" I looked, but I could not see anything at first. It was quite a big sea. Then again she said, "Look there" By this time it was alongside the boat about fifty feet to the right. It was a small container, just on the surface of the water, about twelve foot by eight foot. It became very visible as we went past it, and as it was picked up by the waves, we reported it over the radio. This was about the sixth report of the thing floating in the water. So you must keep a good lookout all the way across.

As we went into our last night I wanted to get a good night's sleep, as I wanted to be fresh to party the next day. I decided that I would go on the 8 till 12 shift, Eric was to do the 12 till 4 and Bob 4 till 8. Then I would come back on to take us in. It was a perfect night, 15 knots of NE trade winds and nice and clear. Eric came on as planned at 12 o'clock. I went to bed at 1.30. I heard a banging noise which sounded like it was coming from the back of our bed. I thought it could only be the rudder. I was quickly getting dressed. The noise changed to a grinding sound which sounded like a motor.

I knew then that it was definitely a steering problem. When I got up top I switched off the Autohelm and the noise stopped. Colette had also got up at the same time. I asked her to do a fix. She gave me our position and told me we had sixty two miles to go. I went down and checked under our bed to see whether or not we had any water coming in the boat from the rudder stock. luckily we were dry. I switched back on the Autohelm only to find the noise starting again. At first, I thought, "Oh good. It's only the Autohelm that has gone." But then I realised that the rudder was stuck and that was what had caused the gears in the Autohelm to go. I tried to turn the wheel, but it was very, very tight. I did not want to force it as we have cable steering and I did not want to snap a cable. The boat seemed to hold a fairly good course, maybe 25-30° off, but that did not bother me as that was Martinique. So I decided to just let the boat go where it wanted without putting any strain on the steering. We had plenty of sea room and were not in any danger.

As the light of the morning came up, Bob had come up to do his shift. I saw a fast fin go down the side of us, and then another and another. We were surrounded by lots and lots of sharks. With only fourty miles to go, I thought surely it can't all go wrong now. But the sharks quickly went; they were just being nosey.

This was probably the first morning the sun had not come up. There were plenty of dark clouds and rain around. With only twenty five miles to go now, I was trying to steer the boat to point a little bit, but it was very tight. I radioed the Catamaran that had been with us the last few days and told them we had a steering problem. They offered to come back for us. I told them that we were OK as the boat was now heading for St. Lucia. About two hours later, we got our first sighting of land.

It is a fantastic feeling to do nearly three thousand miles and end up in the right place. But then again, we have it easy nowadays. I have the greatest respect for the sailors who sailed across years ago without GPS or any other electronic aids. As we got to five miles off, we radioed Arc control to give our ETA of 12 o'clock. The boat just happily continued on with the rudder stuck. We were just pinching a little bit at a time, treating her with tender loving care. As we got to the side of Pigeon Island, it was now time to work out how we could get the boat to turn, other wise we would be going straight past. As we got a mile away, we managed to turn the boat with great care and using the bow thruster we headed for the finish line. It was a fantastic feeling, crossing the line, and there were boats coming out to meet us. We made our way up into the marina, with the bow thruster, so as not to use the steering. We were met on the jetties by locals and Arc officials and friends from the other Arc boats and the party had started. We had a great day.

The next day, I decided to have a good look at our steering, only to find that one of the cables had frayed and was hanging on by one or two strands. It was a good job we hadn't tried to force it. I changed the cable and she is now back as good as new, if not better. My friend Eric was right when we left Las Palmas and he said the steering felt heavy.

One of the first things we did when we arrived was to ring our son and my father. I said, "Dad, We've arrived" "I know." he said, " I've been getting Internet reports every day" At 85 years of age my father had now become an armchair sailor. We partied the rest of that week with all the other Arc boats and then went home for Christmas and New Year. We are now back in the Caribbean, making our way north to the British Virgin Islands.

I would like to take this opportunity to thank you for buying and reading this book. I have to tell you that crossing the Atlantic, for me, was probably the most rewarding thing I will ever do and I think I'll finish where I started by saying, "It's funny but it's true."

Since returning back to England, Dave and Collette have donated a large amount of money to fund the Glaciere of Liverpool project which is a Tall ship berthed in the Albert dock, Liverpool which teaches young people to sail and dive. All funds received from the sale of 'It's funny but it's true', have also been donated to the project. If somebody gave you a copy of this book and you enjoyed the read and would like to make a small donation, we would very much appreciate it.

Thanks,
Dave Murray.

Glaciere of Liverpool
271 South Ferry Quay
Liverpool
L3 4EE

Alternatively, to let Dave know you support the project you can give a donation by credit card by ringing Dave on 07901914499.

Thank you very much, we hope you enjoyed the read!

www.glaciere.co.uk